By the

SIDE

of the

ROAD

THE TRUE STORY OF THE ABDUCTION AND MURDER OF ANN HARRISON

MARLA BERNARD

WILDBLUE
PRESS

WildBluePress.com

BY THE SIDE OF THE ROAD published by:
WILDBLUE PRESS
P.O. Box 102440
Denver, Colorado 80250

WILDBLUE PRESS is registered at the U.S. Patent and Trademark Offices.

ISBN 978-1-957288-49-9 Hardcover
ISBN 978-1-957288-48-2 Trade Paperback
ISBN 978-1-957288-47-5 eBook

Cover Design / Interior Formatting by Elijah Toten
www.totencreative.com

By the
SIDE
of the
ROAD

TABLE OF CONTENTS

FOREWORD

By far, the hardest crime story I've put down on paper has been Ann Harrison's. The six degrees of separation were short skips rather than giant steps to follow. It might be because, in this case, her parents are friends of ours. David served on the police reserves with Bob Harrison. We consider their family as an extended part of our own family. Ann's killers abducted her on David's birthday, which had fallen during Holy Week that year. Police recovered her lifeless body on Holy Thursday. We attended her wake on Easter Sunday. It was a stark and painful contrast to the Mass of Resurrection we had taken part in a few hours before. Seeing a dead child, no matter what the cause, is tragic. Witnessing the pain her parents experienced because of the unspeakable violence that befell their oldest child drives a knife into your gut. No parent should ever have to experience such a tragic and indescribable loss.

Case file information, correspondence to execution witnesses, confession transcripts in their entirety are a part of this book. It is fact-based, supported by this information, so there is no question regarding the story's authenticity.

My husband and I witnessed both of her killers' executions, undertakings that one could only carry out for the most cherished companions on this journey called life. Because of what the Harrisons had endured, it was a simple gesture to walk the last steps on the long road leading to the final chapters in each of the killers' lives. We did so with no compulsion and no regret.

There is a contemporary song that says, "When you're fifteen, and you only have a hundred years to live..." Unfortunately, fate denied Ann the prospect of more than the 5,000 days she lived. Her murderers stayed on death row for twenty-six years—a quarter of a century. It is mind-boggling to attempt reasoning why that happened. Perhaps by telling her story, it will be as though Ann had a little more time.

✴

"If you wait by the river long enough, the bodies of
your enemies will float by."
— **Sun Tzu**, *Chinese philosopher*

According to ancient Greek mythology, five rivers flow to the area they believed was the afterlife, or what we commonly refer to as Heaven or Hell. First, the River Acheron is the River of Pain or the River of Woes. Acheron is also the major river where Charon, the Ferryman of the Underworld, would transport the souls into the afterlife— good or bad. Next, the "River of Wailing," Cocytus, flowed into the Acheron. Loved ones sat by these rivers to wait and watch their families, friends, and enemies move to the afterworld. Next, the goddess of forgetfulness oversaw the River Lethe, leading to the place where virtuous souls rest in peace for eternity with no memory of earthly pain or suffering. In stark contrast, the River Styx was the river of hatred, often thought to be the route to everlasting torment. Finally, it led to the "River of Fire," Phlegethon, which is considered the place where the worst souls ended up, thus the analogies of hellfire and brimstone we know today.

Bob and Janel Harrison waited by the proverbial river of woe for over twenty-five years. Bonne Terre, Missouri is a small rural town whose primary industry related directly or indirectly to the prison. The road to the death house at Bonne Terre connects country lanes and rural back roads that flowed 290 miles from their eastern Kansas City home to the town whose French name translates to "the good earth." For Ann Harrison's family and friends, the only good that came from the many trips down that road was that it brought into focus the prospects of actually moving forward with the executions as the highway signs came into view.

Those roads would be traveled without a conclusion for a quarter of a century before the Department of Corrections could carry out the death sentences. A great price had long since been paid to the Ferryman by the Harrisons, and it was well beyond the time that two wretched beings took passage down the fabled river of fire.

CHAPTER 1

"So, tell me about this Annie Harrison. She signed up to play for me this spring." The Raytown softball coach inquired about the high school sophomore new to his team as Danny Meng listened on the other end of the phone line. Danny was a fixture in the city of Raytown and, if Coach Meng said a player was right, you could bank on that recommendation. Ann had played for Danny, and he was the one who encouraged her to go with this coach's team on the sign-up night. "Well, Annie isn't the team's best player, but you need her on your team. She's the glue that holds it together. Every team needs an Annie Harrison. She's the daughter that any dad would be proud to have. Trust me. You need her on your team."

Ann Harrison—Annie to those she was close to—had just turned fifteen years old one month before sign-up, and she was looking forward to a new season. Early March and teams were forming, but Annie—the team player, the friend, the universal daughter—would never play for the new coach. She would not play again. She had seen her last season.

Michael Taylor and Roderick Nunley were old friends. Taylor had nine prior felony convictions for burglary, stealing and tampering, and had absconded from the custody of a halfway house in November 1988. Kansas City police had issued a warrant for his arrest on December 1, 1988. Taylor was well-versed in prison and probation operations and escaped custody one more time before his story was over. He still had that outstanding warrant for his arrest when he elected to go on a round-the-clock stealing spree around the eastern Kansas City area with Nunley, a career criminal and a suspect in an unrelated homicide.

The two, who specialized in automobile thefts, were riding in a blue 1984 Monte Carlo SS they had stolen between 1:00 and 3:00 a.m. on Wednesday, March 22, 1989, from outside a residence in Grandview, Missouri, a suburb just south of Kansas City. The weather was mild for late March in Kansas City; the sky was clear and there was a full moon. According to the *Farmer's Almanac*, we call a full moon in March a Worm Moon, but it also bears the dubious name of Death Moon because it is the last full moon of winter. March 22, 1989's full moon was the Death Moon for the events about to transpire.

The two thieves ripped off "T-tops" from vehicles in Raytown, Missouri, just east of the Kansas City border, as they smoked drug-laced cigarettes and drank wine. Then, they moved on to the next city over, Lee's Summit, Missouri, to see what they could find to sell for cash and drugs at a local chop shop they liked to frequent. Those "auto repair" businesses were notorious for dismantling stolen cars and selling parts; having opportunities to purchase "hot" or stolen parts in high demand such as T-tops from chumps like Taylor and Nunley was a bonus for the illicit operators.

In the early morning hours, a Lee's Summit police officer spotted the vehicle's broken taillight and attempted to stop the car. A car chase ensued as Nunley sped up to over 90 miles an hour as they crossed city limits into Kansas City. On East U.S. 50 Highway at Unity Village— the road that separated Lee's Summit from Kansas City— the officer suspended the chase at 3:42 a.m. that Wednesday morning. Police procedures did not allow the pursuit of a vehicle into another jurisdiction just for a traffic infraction. After the nature of all the crimes were revealed, the Lee's

Summit officer suffered tremendously from the "what ifs" that plagued many officers. Had there been probable cause to stop the car, this story would have been only a second-page notation in the local newspaper. Had Taylor not slipped away from the halfway house five months earlier, there would have been no stolen car, no stolen property that led the killers to Ann's neighborhood as they drove around, waiting for the chop shop to open, killing time. However, fate would not be so kind.

On March 22, 1989, at a little before 7:00 a.m., Ann Harrison walked to the end of her driveway on the east side of Kansas City to wait for the bus to take her to Raytown South High School. Her mom had called her on the intercom that connected the family home's first floor with Ann's room. The brown-haired, doe-eyed student set her books and flute case at the end of her driveway. Ann had placed her purse next to them, all items in a neatly stacked pile. The Wednesday before Easter was a cool midwestern morning requiring at least a sweater or light coat. Instead, Ann wore a favorite jean jacket—sporting a collection of souvenir pins—and pink slacks with matching socks, the epitome of 1980s fashion. Less than ten minutes from when she exited the front door, the school bus driver honked the horn to summon the teenager. Janel Harrison, Ann's mother, responded alone to the sound of the horn. No one could locate Ann. She had only been a little over sixty feet from her front door and had been outside just a little over seven minutes.

Janel's first thought was that Ann had gone back into the house, but the teenager was nowhere in sight. Ann was not playing with the family dog in the backyard. Janel went to a neighbor's house to see if Ann had visited one of the neighbor girls who often rode the bus, but the girl's mother had driven her to school that day. It was as though Ann had vanished. Janel was grappling with every mother's worst fear as she returned to the house and phoned Bob

Harrison, her husband and Ann's father. Bob was at work in Overland Park, Kansas, southwest of the state line, but he made it back to the family home at record speed. Janel also called the Kansas City, Missouri Police Department to report Ann's disappearance. Bob would also notify the police, but this call was to his brother, Paul, a captain with the KCPD. In rapid succession, ground and aerial searches for the teenager began in earnest.

Clad in school clothes and her jeans jacket, Ann seemed to have just disappeared. No sound, no visible struggle. As if waiting for her immediate return, Ann's belongings were still stacked carefully by the side of the road. Still, neither searchers, police dogs, nor even the police helicopter could find any sign of where she might have gone. It was a parent's worst nightmare and a frustrating set of circumstances for sex crime investigators who were first handed the case. Ann did not fit the profile for a runaway, and the items she left behind were a sign that she most likely had been abducted. But, as much as it appeared to the contrary, she did not just vanish into thin air on an early spring morning.

Ann was 5' 7" and weighed 135 pounds. Although she was an outstanding athlete, her slender frame would be no match for the adult men who would take her hostage. Her volleyball coach would describe her as "tough, having real grit." Only a few weeks into her fifteenth year, it was perhaps that grit, that determination that allowed this child to negotiate with the terrorists that held her captive. She was a shy child, but she summoned a resilience that few adults could conjure up in the throes of such brutality. Dylan Thomas wrote about death in his verse, "Do Not Go Gentle into That Good Night," encouraging readers to "Rage, rage against the dying of the light." Ann Harrison resisted death with her entire being at a mere fifteen years of age.

A typical all-American girl, Ann was active in sports, the school band, and her church. She held a minor job at the local grocery, sacking food, but still was on the honor roll. Her room was messy, with "neat" belongings. Her disappearance was not the stuff runaways were made of, and nothing appeared out of the ordinary in her room. They placed flyers in storefronts of local businesses and handed them out door to door. Her softball coaches went to truck stops handing out flyers to expand the search area. Quickly, word got out, and a convoy of truckers even responded to the site where Ann had been waiting to offer help and broadcast messages across their CB radios.

By late morning, volunteers placed a flyer with Ann's picture in the local grocery store window where she bagged groceries. The story of the missing teenager was the breaking news lead on every television and radio station. Bob Harrison described Ann to reporters as an honor student who "has been active in sports. Girls' softball, soccer, volleyball. She loves to play sports." Ann's high school friend, David Schesser, was her boyfriend for a little over a year. Unfortunately, David was diagnosed with nerve cancer in his right leg in 1986 and relapsed in August 1988. Ann remained loyal through trips to the hospital and chemotherapy, displaying a maturity far beyond her years. Later, before anyone could arrive in person to break the news, David would learn of Ann's death from the television in his hospital room.

Friends established a rewards fund, and newscasters repeatedly recited the TIPS crime hotline number. The Raytown softball league made a significant, anonymous donation to that reward, hoping the funds would be enough of a temptation for someone to report a potential suspect. Within a week, the TIPS Hotline reward grew from $1000 to $4000. A local company donated $2,000 with the request to remain unnamed, and a private donation of $1000, also anonymous, was added to the reward. People called with the information they claimed to have received through dreams, eavesdropping, clairvoyance, and one claimed his information was directly from God.

In 1988, Kansas City, Missouri's homicide rate ranked ahead of New York City, with 134 homicides that year, or 30 murders per 100,000 residents. Conversely, Raytown, Missouri, was a close-knit, middle-class city of roughly 30,000 in 1989. Violent crimes were rare, and the Raytown, Missouri Police Department's claim to fame was traffic tickets. Ann was a sophomore at the Raytown South High School, and the Harrison residence sat mere blocks from the Raytown city limits. It was a quiet neighborhood where it should be safe to stand in one's front yard.

The human-interest focus of the descriptions of her tidily stacked belongings left behind on the curb and her sweet, unassuming demeanor written in the local papers were, in the late 1980s, a sort of comfort. There was no second-by-second coverage reported by talking heads providing unsubstantiated commentary, the pure supposition of what may or may not have happened in a case. With today's victim-of-the-week coverage on all the news channels and social media, the speculation is a warning sign, an advance obituary in draft form. In Ann's case, there was still an air of hope, a prayer, and a whisper that she might still be alive. However, statistics reveal that if you do not locate a child within one to three hours, they are most likely dead. Timelines increase with age, but not to any significant degree.

By Thursday, the only information of any significance available to share was the description of a potential suspect vehicle driven by "persons of interest." Witnesses described the car as possibly a dark brown two-door Chevy Monte Carlo seen near the area of Ann's disappearance. However, the "close but no cigar" scenario kept law enforcement frustrated; the car turned out to be blue.

On March 23rd, the police interviewed one of Ann's friends at the Raytown South High School. She rode the bus with Ann but didn't wait at the same bus stop. On the day of Ann's disappearance, she just surmised that Ann had missed the bus again. She said that Ann had trouble getting to the stop on time, and Ann's mother now made her go out at 7:00 a.m. to wait at the bus stop, which was directly in front of their residence. It was only the length of a tractor-trailer truck from her front door to the curb where she last stood. She was so close but yet still too far from the safety of her own front door, unable to wrench herself away from the grip of death her abductor's clench maintained.

When asked if she knew if Ann ran away or was unhappy, her friend stated Ann was not a runaway and only seemed sad about her boyfriend, David's, battle with cancer. She said that she and her boyfriend would go with Ann and David to the local mall and movies. Ann didn't like it when her parents limited the number of visits to David but otherwise was a quiet and well-adjusted girl. She indicated that one boy on the bus made vulgar comments to Ann who didn't like it. She also mentioned the names of two boys who worked at the local grocery store with Ann and bothered her sometimes. The interview revealed a couple of individuals to follow up on, but nothing changed the fact that this was not a case of an unhappy girl running from her problems. When detectives followed up on those potential leads, they would find nothing useful.

After that interview, police officers contacted Ann's best friend, Juliet Arndt. Her recollection was the same. Ann was a good girl and a loyal friend. She corroborated the first girl's memory that one boy bothered Ann on the school bus and two boys at the local store where Ann worked. They would bother her once in a while, but nothing significant. Ann was not the type of girl who would run away, and the only thing that Juliet could remember that upset Ann was what officers had already learned; her boyfriend's bout with bone cancer distressed her. Ann would sit with her boyfriend during his chemotherapy treatments, even when he was deathly ill from the poison intended to destroy his cancer cells. If he could tolerate the chemo, she could handle the sickening aftermath. In Ann's world, it was just the right thing to do. That's the person she was. Not only was she a good athlete and a good student, but she was also just a genuinely good kid.

CHAPTER 2

Sergeant Troy Cole from the Homicide Unit worked as the floor supervisor on the 4:00 p.m. to midnight shift. He learned that someone had reported a blue Monte Carlo as an abandoned vehicle. At that time, the Sex Crimes Unit, a part of the Violent Crimes Division, was investigating Ann's case. Also, everyone throughout the department was on high alert for a missing teen, as this type of case had captured the entire city's hearts and attention. It would soon become national news.

Sergeant Cole had extensive experience as a detective and a supervisor in the Violent Crimes Division, precisely nine years dedicated to the Homicide Unit. He had previously led a special task force of eleven detectives to investigate notorious serial killer Robert Berdella. Berdella was dubbed "The Kansas City Butcher" because he routinely dismembered his victims, disposing of their bodies in the trash, and, according to rumor, cannibalized at least one of his victims. Ironically, Judge Alvin Randall, who sentenced Roderick Nunley and Michael Taylor in Ann Harrison's case, also presided over the Berdella case. When Berdella died of a massive heart attack during his incarceration at the Missouri State Penitentiary, Judge Randall stated, "Couldn't have happened to a nicer guy."

Cole had also led the special investigative squad formed to probe into the November 29, 1988 explosion that killed six Kansas City, Missouri firefighters. He directed that task force until the Bureau of Alcohol, Tobacco, and Firearms took it over as a federal crime. A laid-back, easy-going Oklahoma native, the other sergeants gave Cole the nickname "Cornbread." Yet, despite his genial down-home persona, he possessed a vast knowledge of homicides.

At 6:55 p.m. on Thursday, March 23, 1989, the residents of an address on the southeast side of Kansas City had contacted the police dispatcher regarding an abandoned car parked in front of their house. When Officer Tommy Williams arrived, they informed him that the vehicle had been there since about 8:30 a.m. on Wednesday, the day of Ann's abduction. The officer ran the license plate and the dispatcher responded that someone stole it from a Grandview, Missouri apartment complex sometime between 1:00 and 6:00 a.m. on Wednesday. The police had also received a report of another car being stolen from that location the same day. There was now the possibility that the crime scene may have expanded into two vehicles and, perhaps, involved several areas.

Officer Williams had processed the vehicle for fingerprints while the 9-1-1 dispatcher attempted to contact the owner. At approximately 7:40 PM, the owner and her boyfriend responded to Williams's location with the vehicle's keys. Knowing the vehicle's history, the boyfriend opened the hood and poured radiator antifreeze in the radiator overflow container, spilling some on the ground under the car. Just as the vehicle was about to be released, the boyfriend opened the trunk to store the anti-freeze. He jumped back, stating there was a body lying in the trunk. When Officer Williams approached the vehicle's rear, he saw a white female lying partially on her left side, fully clothed, wearing white pants, upper body clothing, and tennis shoes. He had discovered Ann's body. It was now 8:15 pm, and the vehicle was a blue, not brown, 1984 Chevy Monte Carlo.

Officer Williams asked the 9-1-1 dispatcher to have the South Zone sergeant respond to the scene and make the notifications to respond to [the address].

The 9-1-1 dispatcher contacted Cole at the Homicide Unit. It was now 8:20 p.m. She stated officers found a body in a recovered stolen auto. "We think it might be Ann." Cole and Detectives Victor Zinn, Ed Glynn, William R. Martin, Bill Wilson, Joe Chapman, and Reed Buente responded to the scene in south Kansas City. Captain Gary Van Buskirk from the Violent Crimes Division arrived at the scene and called Ann's uncle, Paul Harrison, a captain with the KCPD. Van Buskirk asked him to respond to his location to identify the body. "I am sure this is Ann, and I don't want her parents to see her." When Paul Harrison responded to the scene, he made a cursory identification, taking a quick look, walking away, and saying, "That's her." After a few moments, a visibly shaken Harrison told the officers, "I think I better look again," and after stepping up to the trunk again, said, "Yes, that's her." Van Buskirk approached the distraught man and said, "I guarantee you one damn thing, we're going to solve this case." Ann Harrison was family, and it was personal, as Ann was the child of one of their own and another's niece.

※

Sergeant Cole took control of the scene and started the crime scene investigation. Cole notified the dispatcher that the family had positively identified the victim. Crime Scene Investigators Dodd #1532, Parker #1535, and McMillan #1536 responded to the address and processed the scene. A little after 10:30 p.m., police towed the vehicle for further processing at KCPD's #2 garage.

Lying in the trunk on her side, a small amount of blood was visible around Ann's mouth and nose. Drops of blood were on her slacks. They then towed the vehicle to the police garage with the victim inside the trunk to protect the evidence. Sergeant Steve Wright and Steve Warlen of the Regional Crime Lab assumed the responsibilities for processing the vehicle. Technicians took standards for processing and sweepings collected from the car, recovering vehicle and trunk contents as evidence. The lab used a "Super Glue" technique to lift fingerprints from the vehicle. Detectives recovered her bra, right tennis shoe, and jean jacket from inside the trunk. Her captors would not allow her to get dressed entirely before taking her to the vehicle and killing her. Her killers denied her even a modicum of dignity, even in death. After the body was removed from the car's trunk and transported to the medical examiner's office, the lab determined that she had suffered multiple stab wounds to the chest and neck area and had a large laceration on her throat.

The first of several related to Ann's case, the initial crime scene was located outside on a residential, public street.

Detective McMillan detailed the street description in his report and crime scene drawing:

"The street runs north and is paved with asphalt and has a downward slope from south to north. The road is approximately twenty-four feet wide, with a grassy area on the west side. On the east side of the street is an approximate two-foot grassy area, then a four-feet wide sidewalk, and another grassy area.

The vehicle is a 1984 Chevrolet Monte Carlo SS, blue color, two-door, with Missouri 1989 license #HRH-398. This vehicle was parked on the east side of the Street (sic), facing north, approximately one hundred and forty-five feet north of Longview Road and one hundred and twenty-eight feet south of 114th Terrace. There is a working streetlight near this car, and this streetlight is approximately one hundred and thirty-seven feet south of 114th Terrace and around eleven feet east of the east edge of the street.

The Vehicle Identification Number on the car is IGlAZ3761ER202288. There is a Missouri Inspection Sticker #01438432 on the lower left side of the front windshield. On the bottom right side of the front windshield is a Grandview City Sticker #7494. On the left corner of the rear window is a red color sticker which has printed on it PM Parking Permit and has the number 1699 on it."

⚗

The detectives did as much as they could do that night, chasing down every lead, knocking on doors, wearing out shoe leather as the Murder Squad took over the case.

Little more could be done until then, as what few leads the detectives had vaporized with the morning mist. A floor sergeant handled the primary duties in the Homicide Unit on a particular shift. These included the day shift, evening shift, and the overnight shift affectionately known as "dog watch". These shifts had limited detectives due to scheduled days off, so not every detective assigned to a particular squad worked simultaneously. Those shifts were unequipped to investigate a murder with no known suspect. It was up to the Murder Squad, using the maximum number of human resources—a sergeant and six detectives—to work a case like Ann Harrison's—an actual "who done it." That staffing level was essential because alibis were being developed, evidence was being destroyed, suspects were on the run—time is your enemy. The first 48 hours are critical to an investigation, and the chance of successfully identifying suspects is higher within 72 hours.

Captain Van Buskirk formed the murder squad concept in 1988. Before establishing the Murder Squad, the designated sergeant would pick detectives to create a special investigative team to handle this type of case. The drawback was that the sergeant always selected the best detectives, limiting experience for other detectives and increasing burnout within the Homicide Unit. Besides being assigned to a special squad, the detectives still had to handle in-custody cases, suicides, equivocal deaths, or any other case open to interpretation—anything but natural deaths and assaults.

By developing a dedicated squad plan, the duties rotated among squads, so everyone had the same exposure. Only the detectives assigned to the dogwatch shift did not rotate. Van Buskirk's innovative and involved approach to handling violent crimes was legendary. He was a thorough, no-nonsense leader, admired and respected by those he supervised and who supervised him. Troy Cole described him as "the best police officer I ever knew" and that he "worshipped the ground he walked on." As Cole told it, "If someone didn't like Van Buskirk, it was because that person was lazy or didn't care about the job."

As captain of the Violent Crimes Division, Van Buskirk would arrive early to review investigative reports. By the time his detectives returned to work, he would have read every document relating to each homicide, robbery, or sex crime generated the night before. As a result, Van Buskirk knew as much as his sergeants and detectives about every open case.

Sergeant Pete Edlund was the Homicide sergeant on call when someone abducted Ann. Sergeant Cole handed off the case to him. By the time his 42-year law enforcement career was over, he would have served 14 years overseeing homicides. Edlund was Sergeant Cole's alter-ego—candid, brash, outspoken, loud, and driven—but like Sergeant Cole, he was the consummate professional. Homicide sergeants ensure they secure the scene and gain an understanding of it. They confirm that officers keep any witnesses at the scene, determining who they are and what they know. They bring form, order, and structure to an otherwise chaotic scene when no one is in custody.

To get a break from the daily grind of violence, unspeakable horror, and gruesome crime scenes that murder cases churned up, Edlund had transferred and worked a different assignment for two years before going back to supervisory duties on the legendary "Second Floor" in January 1989. Then, Capt. Gary Van Buskirk brought him back, and the fortuitous nature of that request would reveal itself quickly.

If a field sergeant had a question regarding a crime, any crime, they would call the Second Floor and ask for the homicide sergeant on duty. A homicide sergeant was an oracle, a fount of knowledge that was reliable and consistent.

Edlund was there for a little over a month before he caught the case that would forever change the lives of countless officers who worked so diligently to solve it. Edlund described Van Buskirk as a leader for whom Edlund would march into the jaws of Hell. Edlund was thorough to the point of obsessive about his cases, and the captain knew that, with Edlund in charge, no stone would go unturned. Al DeValkenaere, Bill McGhee, Matt Rog, Garry Wantland, Chris Jefferson, Rick Pilgrim, and Herb Acklin were assigned to Edlund's squad. Each would play a significant role in finding Ann's killers.

CHAPTER 3

When Ann's lifeless body was found in the trunk of that blue, not brown, 1984 Chevy Monte Carlo on March 23, 1989, about 8:15 p.m., she had been missing for 37 hours.

The 1030 squad was working the Murder Squad rotation at the time of the murder. Detectives Al DeValkenaere, Bill McGhee, and Matt Rog responded to the southeast Kansas City address. Sergeant Cole briefed them and noted a second car, a white 1979 two-door Buick Riviera, was stolen from an address in Grandview, Missouri, between 2030 hours on 3/21/89 and 0440 hours 3/22/89. The Grandview Police Department provided copies of both stolen auto reports to include in the Ann Harrison murder case file. This vehicle, too, would become a part of the murder investigation, as it would ultimately prove to be the car driven away by one of the killers as they moved Ann's body in the Monte Carlo. No one knew at the time that, when the killers moved the car with Ann in it, she was still alive and would remain so for the next two hours. Her attackers kidnapped, raped, and stabbed her; then, in the most horrific aspect of this brutal crime, they left her alone in the trunk, to die by the side of the road.

A pickup order for the second stolen auto, the 1979 white Buick Riviera in Missouri, was given to the Communications Unit for an all-car broadcast every thirty minutes until officers found the vehicle. After clearing the crime scene in the early morning hours of March 24th, Sergeant Troy

Cole and Detectives Al DeValkenaere and Matt Rog began searching the areas of south KC and Grandview to find that stolen white 1979 Buick Riviera. There would be no sleep that night as they worked straight through what was now long past dawn; this was the beginning of many a sleepless night for each of those detectives as they plunged into the nightmare that was the murder of Ann Harrison. However, no stone was left unturned, and the sheer determination to locate Ann's killers pushed those investigators to keep going. When Grandview, Missouri, police officers ultimately discovered the vehicle at 129th and Cambridge, the Kansas City, Missouri Police Department had it towed to the KCPD's #2 Garage for crime scene investigators to process.

Reports of car break-ins and suspicious vehicles with unknown occupants watching pedestrians and "casing neighborhoods" came in by the dozens. KCPD officers, Jackson County Sheriff's deputies, and Missouri State Highway Patrol officers conducted canvasses of residential areas and businesses with little new information. Within hours, enough evidence from the abandoned vehicle gave officers an idea of the perpetrators' race and sex, along with a sign that the suspects were experienced in auto thefts. Officers had eliminated several in-custody auto theft suspects through the wonders of forensic science. There was not much pushback to get voluntary hair standards. A charge of auto theft was business-as-usual for most of these individuals. The addition of kidnapping, rape, and murder didn't sit well with those guys. The adage "honor among thieves" applied, even if only for fear of being charged with heinous acts.

When suspects were interviewed, investigators got hair standards, fingerprints, and DNA samples from each. Again, no one seemed to have a problem providing samples.

People continued to offer stories of suspicious cars, folks who did not belong in the area, tales of burglaries, and suspected drug use in parking lots and public spaces. It was a time when no one considered telling what you knew as snitching and law enforcement was not the bad guy; sharing any potential evidence or information was considered the honorable thing to do. No one wanted a killer in their midst, as death should not hang in the air like a specter that moved throughout the neighborhood, tolerated like a lawn that needed mowing.

Broken auto parts, discarded women's clothing, bits and pieces of anything appearing to be related to Ann's murder were reported, documented, and investigated. No proverbial stone went unturned, but nothing of substance regarding Ann's killers panned out. However, a plethora of information came in regarding stolen property, auto thefts, burglaries, and other crimes, with good leads and even actual evidence. Detectives would clear unrelated crimes, and the jails filled up, but there was a killer or killers still lurking whose accommodations at the Jackson County Jail had remained unfilled.

Involuntary guests of the jail had information to share with the detectives, but nothing credible. It's not unusual for inmates to try to cut a deal with prosecutors if they believed it would benefit their cases. Sometimes there are facts, often just snippets of information from the rumor mill, but, more often than not, they simply offer crapshoot guesses based on what they've learned from newspapers, television, and their unsavory practices. These came as no surprise as Ann's kidnapping and murder were the lead stories for every news outlet in the region.

After formulating a plan at the scene, Detective William Wilson and Detective Reed Buente began an area canvass of over fifty residences in the area of 113th to 114th and Ditman Avenue as well as the 8600 block of Longview Road. Still, nothing of use came from those contacts. Patrol officers searched the site for any sign of the other stolen car that might be related to Ann's abduction, but nothing had surfaced yet.

They found an unusual dent on the left rear fender when officers inspected the outside of the blue Monte Carlo, four inches up from the molding strip and five inches back from the left rear wheel well. Looking closer, they discovered it came from the trunk, as though someone pushed it outward. Someone also pried out the driver's door lock.

The vehicle's interior was blue, with cloth bucket seats in the front and a bench seat in the rear. The bench seat appeared to be slightly misaligned, as though it had been dislocated. They found carpeted floor mats in both the front and back of the car. A blue ice scraper was found lying on the floor mat on the right front floorboard. Suggestive of a stolen vehicle, the steering column was broken, and the steering wheel's center horn ring was missing. The ashtray and the cigarette lighter were gone, and the radio, later described by the vehicle's owner as a Kenwood AM/FM stereo cassette player, had been removed. They strung the radio wires across the right side of the center console. Under the right rear floor mat were a black color pin, a single dark color eyeglass lens, and a cassette tape case. An interior car light bulb was lying on the rear floorboard, but they did not find the dome lightbulb and the light cover in the vehicle. An Eddie and the Cruisers cassette tape was lying on the back seat's left side, and someone had hung a yellow lei around the inside rearview mirror. The odometer read 56124.2 miles.

There was a pry mark on the left door, and the rubber door molding appeared to have been cracked.

Detective Dodd and Detective McMillan of the CSI Unit responded to the crime scene, photographed the scene, and recovered some evidence from the car. The following is an excerpt from the report taken by Detective McMillan:

"Directing my attention on to the trunk of this vehicle, which was observed open upon our arrival. The victim was lying partially on her back and left side up against the rear of the trunk.

The victim's head was pointed west, and her right leg was straight and pointing northeast. The left leg was bent at the knee with the foot pointing east. The victim's left arm was extended out and bent at the elbow with the left hand pointing to the west. The right arm was laying across the victim's chest. Both the victim's hands appeared to be stained with apparent blood. The victim's face was observed to be partially stained, also, with apparent blood. The victim was wearing a maroon color (sic) long sleeve (sic) sweater that was pulled up just underneath her breasts which exposed her stomach area. On the left side of her stomach were observed blood smears. The victim was wearing light pink color (sic) slacks that had a medium pink colored belt that was undone. The slacks were observed to be zipped up.

Dirt smears were observed on the right leg of the victim's slacks. There were also apparent blood smears on the right front pocket and right front leg of these slacks. On the victim's right foot were two pairs of socks, with the inside sock being a dark pink color and the outside sock being a light pink color. On the left foot were the same socks, but this foot had a white tennis shoe on it. An apparent bruise was observed on the victim's right shin.

Also, in the trunk, and laying under the upper body of the victim, was a green color canvass (sic) tarp which was partially covered with apparent blood. Laying under the victim's right hand was a white-colored bra, which was partial up (sic) covered with apparent blood. Laying over part of the victim's left: (sic) arm was a Stonewashed (sic) jean jacket. Next to the jean jacket was a white color (sic) tennis shoe which still had the shoelaces tied. Laying under the tennis shoe was a white clothing hanger that has a round cardboard bottom that also had an apparent blood smear on part of it. There was a closed purple color (sic) umbrella lying next to the Inside (sic) of the victim's leg. Lying next to the outside of the victim's right leg was a card board (sic) car window sunscreen. Next to this was a plastic bottle of windshield washer fluid.

The spare tire was observed to be securely fastened to the right side of the trunk. The entire floor of the trunk was covered with a black color (sic) trunk mat. A white color metal—(sic) type button with "Disneyland" on it was found under the jean jacket. On the front wall of the trunk is an unknown type of e (sic) matting that separates the trunk from the back seat. On the right side of this matting were five noticeable gouge marks. On the left side of this matting were three noticeable gouge marks. On the trunk lid was an apparent dirt smear that was approximately six inches in from the left edge and was in the center of the trunk lid, running from front to rear. Near the rear of the trunk lid approximately twelve inches in from the left edge of the trunk lid, was an unknown white substance. Approximately three inches from this was what appeared to be a fresh scratch in the paint. On the right side of the trunk lid, approximately twelve inches in from the right side, was an unknown white substance. On the right side of the rubber trunk molding was observed an unknown type of red color (sic) fabric. In the left side and the right side of the water drain channel that runs around the trunk were observed an unknown type of light brown color (sic) tree bugs.

A partial shoe impression was found on the left side of the rear bumper. On top of the plastic cover for the license plate and gas tank filler were some type of fabric impressions in the dust. It should be noted that the vehicle was towed to the Number Two garage (sic) for the majority of this crime scene processing. The car was left in the garage paint room for further examination by the Regional Crime Lab."

CHAPTER 4

By 7:00 a.m. on March 24th, Matt Rog and Al DeValkenaere had conducted a roadblock at 114th and Ditman Avenue to glean any potential witness information from drivers who may have seen the car.

Later that day, detectives contacted the owner of the Monte Carlo. They asked if she recalled anything missing from her Monte Carlo from the previous night, hoping she would remember something she might not have recognized at the scene.

She described her car's interior and exterior portions as having been in excellent condition. The vehicle's dome light lens, cigarette lighter, ashtray, center horn piece, radio, and gas cap were all intact when she drove it last. She noted that her center console contents included: an *Eddie and the Cruisers* cassette tape, a *Tiffany* cassette tape, a *Dirty Dancing* cassette tape, safety goggles, a red hairbrush, a brown book in which she kept the vehicle's mileage and gas log, and $4.00 in quarters. In addition, she stated her glove box contained a map, insurance papers, and a silver flashlight with a yellow button that turns it on and off. She also said she had hung a yellow lei over her interior rearview mirror.

[The previous owner] stated there had not been previous damage to the trunk, and the trunk contained a green canvas tarp, a purple umbrella, a bottle of windshield cleaner, and a cardboard window sunscreen. She did not remember a white metal button with Disneyland inscribed on it anywhere in the car but said perhaps her boyfriend might have given a button like that to one of her children at one time.

She stated she would assist the police any way she could but was afraid and had moved in temporarily with her boyfriend's mother, who lived in Belton, providing both a contact address and phone number to the detectives.

On Thursday night, detectives interviewed a classmate of Ann's when he reported passing a fast-moving vehicle driving down Manchester with Ann in the front seat. He stated it was a blue or black General Motors car, and he remembered it because he had to swerve his vehicle to avoid hitting it. He noted a white male and a black male were in the car, and it was early morning, between 7:00 and 7:15 a.m.

He indicated that, later in the day, he saw the police tow the vehicle "today" (3/23/89) escorted by motorcycle officers in front of and behind the car, and it was the same one he had seen on Manchester. He was adamant that Ann had attended the same school and worked at the same grocery store. He could not identify either male occupant as anyone he knew or had seen before but described Ann's jacket and said her hair looked wet. When officers asked why none of this was reported on the day she went missing, he stated he gave information to some officers who came to Ann's place of work but felt that his statement "was just blown off." He could provide no specific information about the officers he discussed this information with or any other details about his report. He came forward to the KCPD when his dad told him that Ann had been found dead inside the vehicle's trunk.

Officers could not corroborate the student's story, nor was any information he claimed he gave to officers ever substantiated. Despite the gaps in his story, the student would not back down, insisting that the suspects were black and white males. Officers would spend far too many precious hours running down a story that contained inaccuracies that complicated an already complicated case.

✳

On March 24, 1989, the members of the Center Zone Tactical Squads 160 and 170, each with a sergeant and six officers, responded to police headquarters at 0900 hours to be briefed on the Ann Harrison case. They then reassembled at the Longview Lake marina and searched for a crime scene. The teams explored all 14 shelter houses and the surrounding areas, and the beach area, the soccer pitch, and the ball fields were all searched. Officers found nothing of any substance despite their best efforts.

The plan extended into the Cave Springs Nature Preserve, the Navajo Lake area, and Swope Park—a park second only to New York City's Central Park in expanse—requiring multiple agencies to help cover such a massive amount of ground. Members of the Jackson County Sheriff's Office assisted in the search. First, all the adjacent spaces were checked, including dead ends and side streets, but they found nothing of any significance. Next, an area between 63rd Street to the north and 87 Street to the south, east to Blue Ridge, were checked with negative results. Then, they walked the railroad tracks that run north and south along Oldham Road. Again, searchers could find no evidence of a crime scene anywhere.

Detective Garry Wantland contacted the Longview Parks Department to determine if they would collect trash in the Longview Lake area. Nothing was removed, and no one had policed the areas since March 20th. The supervisor indicated he would not allow staff to do either until after the KCPD had released the site. They would have staff block off any roads around Longview Lake to assist police with the investigation.

Later that day, detectives responded to Longview and Ditman Avenue to conduct an area search with the help of the Missouri Search and Rescue K-9 Unit to check the neighboring areas. Before meeting the canine team, one detective checked the victim's blue jean jacket out of the Crime Lab, using it as a starting scent for the tracking dogs. The canines show that the smell proceeded eastbound on Longview to Raytown Road, then northbound on Raytown Road.

Upon arriving at 109th and Raytown Road, the dogs located two scents on 109th Street, one proceeding eastbound and the other westbound. The canines indicated the scene moved approximately one quarter of a mile east on 109th Street and then off the roadway on the south side of the street to a wooded area and the edge of Longview Lake. The canines then proceeded westbound on 109th to Raytown Road, northbound on Raytown Road to 83rd Street, westbound on 83rd Street to James A. Reed, and northbound from James A. Reed to Blue Ridge. The search would continue the following morning because it was getting dark and for fear of exhausting the canines. Detectives returned the blue jean jacket to the Crime Scene Investigations Unit, securing it back into evidence.

Concerning the stolen auto in Grandview, DeValkenaere, Rog, McGhee, and Wantland conducted an area canvass of apartments in the 6100 block of E. 127th with the help of Detective Terry Barnes of the Grandview PD. The detectives hoped to gain possible suspect information, but those hopes were dashed once again.

The day after Ann's body was recovered, Detectives Rick Pilgrim and Herb Acklin began the first of many area canvasses to locate witnesses who may have possible information about her abduction and murder. They started by re-canvassing the 6700 and 6800 blocks of Manchester. With no results, they then moved to 6800 and 6900 Manchester. No one had any additional information of benefit. The area produced no valuable leads. The next day, they began again, moving to the 6400 and 6600 blocks of James A. Reed Road. Still, no witnesses offered anything useful to solving the crime.

CHAPTER 5

The following are excerpts from the investigative reports from March 24, 1989, regarding the processing of evidence in this homicide case. The investigations were conducted at the Jackson County Medical Examiner's office, at the Truman Medical Center Morgue at 2301 Holmes Road in Kansas City, Missouri. All the documentation was reviewed and approved by Sergeant Pete Edlund.

Detective James Shea of the Robbery Unit documented the initial body examination.

"On 3-24-89, at 0108 hours, the reporting officer in company with Detective Jon Jacobson responded to the Truman Medical Center Morgue, 2301 Holmes, where a body examination was conducted on the above captioned (sic) victim, Ann M. Harrison.

The victim was noted to be laying (sic) supine on a cart in the Truman Medical Center Morgue with her arms crossed over her torso and her left leg bent outward at the knee. The victim had a brown hair barrette (sic) in her hair, a gold necklace around her neck (sic) and was wearing a maroon sweater, no bra, a pair of pink pants, white underpants, pink socks, and a white tennis shoe on her left foot. The right shoe was missing. The victim also had brown paper bags covering her hands. The bags were secured in place by evidence tape. It should be noted that the top button of the pink pants was missing and the pink cloth belt, which was part of the pants, was unbuckled.

Rigor was pronounced and livor was noted on the left side of both breasts, the left side of the back, the left buttock, the outside of the left thigh and the inside of the right thigh. The Victim's Face (sic) and hands were covered with what appeared to be dried blood. The. victim's hands were clutched (sic) and in her right hand were what appeared to be several hairs.

The following wounds were noted to the victim:

#1. Incised wound under the chin, one quarter inch long, one and one quarter inches right of midline and four and one-quarter (sic) inches above the supia sternal notch (sic).

#2. Puncture wound to the right side of the neck, three quarters inch in diameter, three and one inches right of midline and two and one quarter Inches (sic) below the right earlobe.

#3 Incised wound to the front of the neck one and three-eighths inches long, three inches above the supia sternal notch (sic) beginning at midline and extending horizontally one and three-eighths inches to the right of midline.

#4 Incised stab wound to the chest three quarters inch in length by three-sixteenth (sic) inches wide, two and one-half inches left of midline and three and one-half inches below the supia sternal notch (sic).

#5 Incised stab wound to the chest, one quarter inch long, one inch left of midline and five and three-quarters inches below the supia sternal notch (sic).

#6 Incised stab wound to the chest, three-quarters (sic) inch long by one-quarter (sic) inch wide, one and one-quarter inches left of the midline and six and one-quarter inches below the supia sternal notch (sic).

#7 Incised stab wound to the right side of the chest, one-half (sic) inch long, seven inches right of midline and six and one-half inches below the right arm pit.

#8 Incised stab wound to the right side of the chest, one-half (sic) inch long, nine inches right of midline and six and one-quarter inches below the right arm.

#9 Incised stab wound three-quarter (sic) inch long, three inches right of midline and twelve inches below the base of the right shoulder.

It should be noted that the victim also had a small bruise approximately one-half (sic) inch in diameter on the shin of her right leg, midway between the knee and the ankle. Just below this bruise was a bruise approximately three inches long by one inch wide, which began in the center of the right leg and extended outward. It should also be noted that a piece of brown unknown debris was recovered from the victim's upper right back."

Detective George Barrios of the Homicide Unit recorded the autopsy that was conducted.

"On 03-24-89, at 0700 hours, Detective David Ray and I observed Dr. Bonita Peterson conduct an autopsy on the listed homicide victim at the Truman Medical Center Morgue. During the course of the autopsy (sic) blood was drawn from the victim and blood was put into a gray topped glass tube, and a blue topped glass tube. Two vital (sic), two oral (mouth) and two vaginal swabs were also Obtained (sic). Rectal, vaginal and oral slides were obtained from the victim. A section of the victim's ribs was also obtained from one area where she was apparently stabbed. A silicone knife blade impression was taken from the victim's liver by Ralph Blainy of the Regional Crime Lab. The tubes of blood, the slides, the swabs (sic) and the silicone impressions of a knife blade were hand carried to the Regional Crime Lab."

In his confession, Taylor claimed that he "didn't finish," but blood-typing and DNA testing of semen found in the victim's genitals and on her clothing established that the source of the semen was Taylor. As a result of his forcible sexual assault, Ann suffered lacerations to her vagina.

While Ann Harrison, bound and blindfolded, lay in the trunk, Nunley went upstairs and got two knives: a large butcher knife and a small, serrated steak knife; he gave Taylor the steak knife and kept the butcher knife for himself. According to Taylor's statement to police, Nunley urged they kill the victim to prevent her from identifying him. Taylor was reluctant to take part because Ann had not seen Taylor. By Taylor's account, Nunley grabbed the victim's neck and attempted to cut her throat, but the butcher knife was too dull, producing only scratches on her throat. Nunley then stabbed Ann Harrison through the throat and chest, while Taylor stabbed her two to four times in the torso. The victim's autopsy revealed stab wounds to her chest, side, and back, penetrating her heart, lungs, and other internal organs, and more stab wounds to her neck. After the stabbing, Taylor watched for a time as Ann Harrison lay in the trunk and futilely struggled to breathe through her damaged lungs.

Ann Harrison died from her many stab wounds, especially those that penetrated her heart. Ann remained alive during the stabbing while they inflicted her with ten wounds, remaining conscious for 15 minutes after being stabbed. She would live for two more hours, alive in the trunk as the car she lay in sped away to be discarded at what was then an unknown location.

Detective D.W. Atchison of the Homicide Unit wrote the following report when he met with Detectives Shea and Jacobson at the medical examiner's office to conduct the postmortem body examination on Ann Harrison.

"Upon arrival, the victim's body was observed lying on a cart, face up, wrapped in a white body shroud. The victim's hands (sic) bagged, and she was wearing the following clothing items. (Maroon sweater, light pink pants, dark pink

and light pink socks on both feet, white athletic shoe on left foot, gold color necklace surrounded by white stones and a silver hair clip). The victim's pants had a cloth-type belt which was undone and the top button on the fly was also undone.

The aforementioned bags covering the victim's hands were removed at which time both of the victim's hand (sic) were observed to be bloodstained. Hairs and/or fibers were collected from both of the victim's hands as well as fingernail scrapings. Apparent bloodstains were observed on the victim's pants and panties in the vaginal area.

Loose hair was collected from the left front side of the sweater, back (sic) and chin area. An unknown debris item was collected from the upper right rear shoulder blade area of the victim's back.

Regional Crime Lab personnel, Chemist John Wilson, collected swabbings of both the right and left breasts of the victim.

Pubic hairs were collected which appeared to have an unknown substance attached to them. A pubic hair combing as well as a standard was collected. Victim's head hair standard was also collected.

The following wounds were observed on the victim's body:

1). Incised stab wound: (1/4") length, (3/16") wide, (2-1/2") left of midline, (3 ½") below supra sternal notch (sic). (Left breast area)

2). Incised stab wound: (3/4") length, (3/16") wide, (1-1/2") left of midline, (6 1/4") below supra sternal notch (sic). (Left breast area)

3). Puncture wound; (3/4") diameter, (right side of neck), (3-1/2") right of midline, (2-1/\4") below right earlobe.

4). Incised stab wound; (front of neck), (1-3/8") length, (3") above supra sternal notch (sic), horizontal, beginning at midline to (1-3/8") right.

5). Incised stab wound: (1/4") length, (1") left of the midline, (5-3/4") below supra sternal notch (sic). (Left breast area).

6). Incised stab wound; (1/2") length, (7") right of midline, (6-1/2") below right arm pit (Right side of body)

7). Incised stab wound; (1/2") length, (9") right of midline, (6-1/4") below right arm pit (Right side of body)

8). Incised stab wound; (3/4") length, (3") right of midline, (12") below base of right shoulder (Back of victim (sic) right shoulder)

9). Incised stab wound; (1/4") length, (1-1/4") right of midline, (4-1/4") above supra sternal notch (sic). (Under right chin area).

Lividity was observed on the victim's left side of back, buttocks, thigh (sic) and inside portion of right thigh. Lividity was also observed on the inner midline portion of the victim's right breast.

Bruising was observed on the victim's right shin area.

A smear type (sic) pattern of blood was observed on the left side of the victim's face which was closely photographed.

The victim's left shoe was processed for fingerprints at which time one latent card of lifts were recovered. This card and two sets of victim's eliminations were recovered from the victims' (sic) body and were sent to the Fingerprint ID Section.

All aforementioned items of evidence collected were packaged and sent to the Regional Crime Laboratory for processing with the exception of the fingerprint items."

✳

While the medical examiner conducted the autopsy, the police dispatcher notified detectives that a car, reported stolen between 8:30 p.m. on 3/21/89 and 5:00 a.m. on 3/22/89, a white 1979 two-door Buick Riviera, was stolen from a residence in Grandview, Missouri and was later recovered at 129th and Cambridge. The location and time frame of this auto theft was eerily like the theft of the vehicle that held Ann's body. Crime Scene detectives responded to photograph the car and conduct some initial processing before towing it to the KCPD #2 garage for processing.

The vehicle was a two-door Buick Riviera, with a white vinyl top. There was a pry mark on the door similar to the one found on the blue Monte Carlo, and it damaged the steering column on the left side of the column. Shoe impressions were found on paper lying on the passenger side of the front floor.

The interior was red velour with a split-bench front seat. The steering column displayed damage along the left side of the column, and the dome light had been removed. A glass "T" top was found in the back seat. All the damage to the vehicle was in keeping with the observations made on the blue Monte Carlo.

✳

On March 25, 1989, the *Kansas City Star* newspaper published Ann Harrison's obituary. It read as follows:

Services for Ann Marie Harrison, 15, east Kansas City (sic) who was found dead March 23, 1989, in southeast Kansas City, will be at 10 a.m. Monday at Blue Ridge Presbyterian Church, burial in Mount Olivet Cemetery, Raytown. Friends may call from 2 to 7 p.m. Sunday at the Sheil Colonial Chapel. The family requests no flowers and suggests contributions to the Lost Child Network 8900 State Line Road Leawood, or the Dream Factory, OFFICER Box 12373, North Kansas City. Ann was born in Kansas City. She was a freshman honor student at Raytown South High School, where she was a member of the volleyball team and the freshmen (sic) band. She was a member of the Raytown Girls Softball League and the Raytown Girls Basketball League. She was a member of the Blue Ridge Presbyterian

Church. Survivors include her parents, Mr. and Mrs. Robert Harrison, and two sisters, Debra Harrison and Lisa Harrison, all of the home; her paternal grandfather, Phil Harrison, Raytown; and her maternal grandparents, Mr. and Mrs. Ivan Schinkle, North Hollywood, Calif.

⁜

On March 26, 1989, Grandview Police notified the Homicide Unit that their officers were involved in a car chase from High Grove and Donnelly, in Grandview, Missouri, to a residence on Herrick. The vehicle, a green 1980 Chevrolet Citation, four-door, with a Missouri license plate, was abandoned at that location, and the suspects fled the scene. License WC-057, Missouri '90, had been recovered at the Herrick residence after the suspects had fled the vehicle and were still at large. Homicide detectives responded to the scene and contacted a Grandview, Missouri police sergeant who advised them that this vehicle had been involved in auto thefts at Skate Land (no longer in business), on South 71 Highway. He had located it in Grandview and chased it into Kansas City, Missouri. The suspects, two black males, jumped from the car, and ran westbound from the scene. When the sergeant approached the abandoned Chevy, he saw what appeared to be a stolen vehicle because the steering column was broken.

The door cylinder lock on the car's front passenger side had a pry mark. It looked like someone stuck a screwdriver under the door cylinder to break it. In addition, someone had pulled the car radio from the wiring and placed it on the passenger-side floorboard. As in the Ann Harrison case, the inside dome light had the outer plastic cover removed, and the lamp's bulb was missing. All this damage and the broken steering column were consistent with the vehicle in the homicide case. The Grandview Police concurred with the detectives' observations based on this information. The police towed the car to KCPD's #2 garage to allow crime scene investigators to process it and compare it to the information from the vehicle where Ann's body was found.

Grandview police officers responded to a residence on East 128th Terrace for a reported stolen vehicle the following day. It was the one that officers had recovered from the car chase. Detectives were unsure what they had, but they knew the occurrences set a pattern. Their investigation seemed less coincidental. Ann's killers were still out there, similar car thefts were occurring, and it appeared that the suspects were circling the area like a kettle of vultures, hovering above potential prey.

✻

It was March 29th, a few hours before dawn, when officers began contacting employees at 24-hour businesses to determine if there was anyone who recalled observing a vehicle matching the description of the 1984 Monte Carlo SS. Out of the fourteen separate employees checked, only the employee of a 7-11 on Bannister thought he saw the vehicle but could not describe the occupants.

During that same time frame, troopers from the Missouri Highway Patrol's Troop canvassed all of Lee's Summit businesses open in early morning hours. Eight locations were open at that time; they showed a photo of the blue 1984 Monte Carlo SS to the employees, but no one recalled seeing that vehicle.

Later that same day, detectives conducted yet another roadblock at 68th and Manchester to stop all vehicular and foot traffic to show pictures of the Monte Carlo to see if anyone might have seen the car when Ann was abducted. But, once again, no new leads were generated, despite their best efforts.

One week after the abduction, Detectives McGhee and Wantland responded to an address on 103rd and Oakland

and contacted a gentleman who witnessed property damage to a vehicle shortly after midnight on March 22nd. The owners reported the damage to police later, corroborating the other statement. The property damage involved a white Buick Riviera that two black male suspects were occupying. Thieves had stolen a white Riviera from the same area and in the same time frame as the stolen Monte Carlo.

The caller told the detectives that he observed the white Riviera occupied by two black males traveling south on Oakland and stopping in front of a residence on Oakland. He then saw the Riviera back up and stop in front of a nearby residence also on Oakland. He watched as the front passenger exited the Riviera while the driver remained seated in the car. The passenger then approached a truck parked in the driveway of that residence and broke out the truck's side wing vent window with an unknown object. He said that he then turned on his porch light and closed his front door to scare the suspects away. At that point, the passenger then ran away from the truck and back to the Riviera, jumped into the passenger seat, and the vehicle then headed south on Oakland at a high rate of speed.

The caller then ran outside and observed a black male driving the Riviera. He described the passenger as a black male about 6 feet tall, thin, and wearing a dark baseball hat or stocking cap and a dark coat.

Detectives showed the caller four photographs of the Riviera stolen from the area around the same time as the Monte Carlo. He positively identified the vehicle as being the one he observed. He noted that he initially reported to the police that the suspect vehicle involved in the property damage case was a later model Riviera. He knew the car he had seen had a brake light in the rear window, and he did not know that the older (1979) Riviera had a brake light in the back window. The gentleman told detectives he did not believe he could identify the two black males if he saw them again. It connected a few more lines to map out where the suspects may have been, but still nothing concrete.

✳

The next day, a woman provided information to homicide detectives following up on her report to police regarding a car being driven erratically on 350 Highway and Blue Ridge before it turned off Blue Ridge and headed west on 67th Street. She described two black males, one of whom wore a black baseball cap. She said it was hard to get a good look at the driver but that the passenger appeared to be in his twenties, light-skinned, and clean-shaven. She estimated that the incident took place at about ten minutes before 7:00 a.m. because she arrived at her office at 63rd and Raytown Road 5 minutes later at 5 minutes before 7:00 a.m. Unfortunately, she could not get a license number.

Calls continued to come in with no substantial leads. One report stated that a satanic cult was responsible. Rumors claimed there were stab marks on the body in a satanic design. How stab wounds of any type were common knowledge five days after the killing was anyone's guess. Bearing in mind that this was long before the days of social media, bad news still traveled fast. Customers at a local drinking establishment claimed to have overheard a conversation by questionable-looking characters discussing crimes concerning themselves. "You should not have killed that girl." Secondhand information proved to be just another dead end on this endless highway of misinformation; hearsay was the subject of the day. The intelligence proved to be helpful in unexpected and unrelated ways. Helpful information on unrelated crimes came in, but nothing helped the detectives move the crystal ball forward. Both sides of the state line reported leads, and detectives followed each one. It was a massive undertaking; this was a case that locals would remember for decades to come.

CHAPTER 6

Several local high school administrators reported information brought forth from students. A local senior center turned in the name of a person fired from his job for possessing pornographic photos. Another individual shared information on an alleged religious cult in Grandview, Missouri. In addition, there were rumors of a bloody mattress in an abandoned house in Raytown. These were the types of calls that surfaced from TIPS, direct calls to the Homicide Unit, and the 9-1-1 dispatcher.

The TIPS Hotline also received hundreds of calls about known auto thieves. Roderick Nunley's name would surface two months later on the hotline. The Crimes Against Property Unit had also contacted the Homicide Unit to provide the name of an auto thief, whose standard practice matched those of the stolen Monte Carlo. His name was Roderick Nunley.

Leads came in on this and a multitude of other similar crimes. Detectives got head and pubic hair samples and fingerprints given voluntarily by a host of suspects arrested for auto theft, rape, assault, and robbery. These individuals always agreed to provide samples which eliminated them as murder suspects. Auto theft victims also provided fingerprint and hair standards. Detectives hoped that something would break to link the cars together and generate substantial leads.

While Nunley and Taylor were on the street after Ann's murder, numerous recovered and attempted stolen autos displayed the same characteristics found in the stolen vehicles involved in Ann's murder. Nunley and Taylor's trademarks were pry marks on the door locks, the broken steering columns, the missing radio, front ashtray, and dome lights. Taylor had learned his disreputable trade from Nunley, who was notorious for auto thefts in the greater Kansas City area. He made an excellent apprentice felon, studying under a master at his illicit craft. Ironically, by mirroring Nunley's techniques, he would place himself in the crosshairs of the investigators who followed that signature method until they affixed the virtual rifle scope upon both criminals.

On April 17th, detectives DeValkenaere and Wantland headed to the address on 118th Place. They learned that Officer David Ferber was at that location regarding another stolen auto he thought might interest them. The 1986 white Chevrolet Cavalier, two-door, had been stolen from an address on E. 54th Street on April 15th. The damage to the vehicle was consistent with the damage to the car involved in the Harrison investigation.

Someone had attempted to remove the lock cylinder on the driver's door. The steering column was broken, the interior dome light was removed, and the ashtray was missing from the vehicle. These were all Taylor and Nunley's trademarks. When the car was towed to the Kansas City Police Service Station for processing by CSI Detective Hattaway, he found the car was "wiped clean" apparently by the suspect or suspects, just like in the Harrison case. Hattaway could recover no prints of value.

A check of stolen auto reports showed that on April 22, police recovered a vehicle at 51st and Myrtle, within blocks of where Michael Taylor lived. Someone had stolen it during an armed robbery at an address on Prospect, and police could lift latent prints from the automobile. The 1976 Cadillac was missing tires, wheels, the front grill, the radio, and speakers. A T-top was lying in the back seat, and the ashtray was missing. Detectives could attribute this type of work to Taylor and Nunley, and the list of comparable crimes continued to grow.

By April 18th, Ralph Baney, the Regional Criminalistics Laboratory Forensic Firearms & Toolmark Examiner III, had been given Ann's maroon sweater, her right tennis shoe, two knives, and silicone casts of the knife impression of her liver, and a section of the victim's ribs for analysis; a gruesome, yet tragic, assortment of evidence to examine.

During the first week of May, Grandview Police contacted the KCPD Homicide Unit about another stolen auto found in their city limits at an address on E. 125th Street. The car was a maroon 1985 Chevrolet Monte Carlo SS, with the dome light removed and a broken steering column on the left side. In addition, the radio was gone, the wires were hanging out, and the ashtray was missing. The damage was consistent with the stolen autos that the detectives had located and processed concerning Ann's case.

The owner reported this vehicle stolen from an address on W. 14th Street, Kansas City, Missouri, on May 4th. This information and witness statements that two black males had possibly exited the vehicle made this incident of significant interest. Crime scene detectives from Kansas City responded and processed the vehicle based on this.

In May 1989, a criminal incarcerated in Arizona had contacted Bob Harrison about Ann's murder. Detective McGhee spoke to an agent at the Federal Bureau of Investigation's Arizona office regarding this individual. Unfortunately, he was known for attempting to provide lousy information on cases to get a lighter sentence for his burglary case, so there was no validity to his claims. This unsubstantiated lead was just another setback, a dead-end on the road that, once again, shifted the investigation back into reverse.

CHAPTER 7

Roderick Nunley was a person of interest from early in the case. Officers brought him to the Homicide Unit for questioning twice in May 1989 to get a statement regarding the Ann Harrison case and see if he would allow detectives to take head and pubic hair standards.

Detective Robert Ransburg checked Nunley out of the Jackson County Detention Unit in mid-May. He transported him to the Crimes Against Persons Division, hoping to get Nunley to sign a consent form and allow for the hair standards to be collected. Instead, officers found information that led to the arrest of Nunley for a car theft he had committed in February 1989. The damage Nunley caused in the process of breaking into that vehicle was eerily like the damage found on the Monte Carlo containing Ann's body.

Nunley declined to sign the release or consent to give hair standards, stating he needed to talk to a lawyer first. Officers didn't ask any further; they transported Nunley back to the Jackson County jail. If Nunley had nothing to hide, it would have been in his interest to sign the release and provide hair standards. Perhaps he feared being tied to other stolen autos, or maybe there was more that he was afraid of, but only time would tell.

By the end of May, Nunley was back in jail, this time on a stop order for stealing. Detective DeValkenaere signed Nunley out of the Central Detention Unit, escorting him to the Homicide Unit to question him about the Harrison case.

They immediately advised Nunley of his rights and provided the Miranda Form 340 P. D., which he refused to sign. He told detectives DeValkenaere and Detective McGhee that he would not talk to them without an attorney.

Once again, the detectives had to put Nunley back where they found him, but, at least for a time, they knew where and how to locate him.

Several days later, in June 1989, Nunley described to an acquaintance how he and Taylor had kidnapped a girl named "Annie," raped her, and stabbed her to death. He told the confidant that Taylor always wanted to have sex with a white girl and that grabbing Ann was Taylor's idea. Nunley's friend claimed that he, Nunley, said he only wanted to steal auto parts so that he could sell them for cash or drugs.

A little before noon on June 21, 1989, an anonymous tip about the murder of Ann Harrison came in on the TIPS Hotline. An anonymous source stated he knew who had killed Ann Harrison. The caller said a Mike Taylor, a black male, 23 years of age, whose mother lives in the 5400 block of Garfield on the east side of the street, in an odd number house, on the south side of the block was the person who raped Ann Harrison. The caller further stated that Mike Taylor was currently in the Missouri State Penitentiary for a parole violation that had recently been served on him. The caller noted that the guy that killed Ann Harrison is Roger Nunley, a black male, 24 years of age, who had just beat a case of murder that occurred at 52nd and Highland and the dead person was a man by the name of Jonas. "Roger" it would later be determined, was a nickname that one of Ann's killers was known by and an alias that would surface in police reports as the case unfolded. The caller stated that Ann Harrison was killed in the basement of Roger Nunley's mother's house in Grandview and that Roger had cut her throat and then made Mike stab her so that he would be part of the murder. The caller further stated that Roger had gagged her mouth at the time of this attack.

The acquaintance informed police of Nunley's story so that he could collect the TIPS Hotline reward that had now increased to $9,000.00. He specifically mentioned the amount when he called in to report Nunley as the killer. The caller stated he would call back on June 22nd at approximately 1:00 p.m.

When the anonymous caller contacted the TIPS Hotline the next day, he identified himself as Kareem Hurley, Roderick Nunley's friend. He agreed to meet with detectives at police headquarters at 3:00 p.m. that same day. As a result, they interviewed Kareem Akbar Hurley at the Crimes Against Persons Division.

Everyone went above and beyond. A quick-thinking TIPS hotline call taker kept tipster Kareem Hurley on the line, convincing him to let the call be transferred to the detectives who were in the homicide unit. DeValkenaere spoke with him, and he mentioned "Annie" and knew details and apparent facts that only the killer knew. He even agreed to come in and meet with detectives to give a statement.

The caller stated that when Roger and Mike abducted Ann Harrison, they only intended to steal Ann's purse; however, they took Ann. The caller indicated that Roger and Mike drove Ann Harrison to Roger's mother's house and had driven into the basement with her in the car. The caller stated officers wouldn't find blood in the basement/garage because they killed her in the trunk.

Detectives confirmed Roger Nunley to be Roderick Nunley, a black male whose date of birth was 03-10-65, and Mike Taylor was Michael Taylor, a black male whose date of birth was 01-30-67. Michael Taylor appeared in Missouri State Penitentiary files showing that police arrested him on a parole violation on March 28, 1989 and sent him back to prison. The computer also showed him to have a previous address on the 5400 block of Garfield. Roderick Nunley, who had an alias of Roger Nunley, was found because he was a suspect in the Jonas Dickerson homicide at 52nd and Highland.

Detective Al DeValkenaere recalled, "The caller stated we could make Mike on pubic hair because Mike was the one that raped Ann; however, Nunley would be a 'hard nut to crack.' The caller advised us to try to get Taylor to talk first. I should note that information relayed from the caller to us was not information ever disclosed to the media, nor was it information that any person other than the killers of Ann Harrison or someone they may have told would know. That information had been held in strict confidence. Only to the detectives assigned to the case knew about it."

Hurley claimed that Roderick Nunley had killed the victim in the basement of Nunley's mother's house. A computer check revealed Nunley's mother, Mattie Nunley, lived at an address on the 7400 block of East 118th Street. The calling party stated that Nunley had told him about the killing, providing details that were not previously released about the crime. The information had to have come from someone involved in the victim's death.

⁜

Case Review sent a detainer to the Department of Corrections on Jackson County Felony warrant #CR89-3324 for First Degree Murder, Armed Criminal Action, Kidnapping, and Rape. Nunley and Taylor would each have a $125,000 bond.

Based on these additional facts, Detectives DeValkenaere and McGhee got a search warrant for the address on the 7400 block of East 118th Street from Jackson County Circuit Court Judge Robert Iannone. After getting the search warrant, the detectives responded to 7405 East 118th Street to execute it.

The first search warrant served on Nunley's mother's house on the 7400 block of E. 118th Street, Kansas City, was executed 6/21/89 at 2000 hours. Mattie L. Nunley, James R. Davis, Leslie Nunley, and Roderick Nunley, all residents at that address, were home. They executed the search warrant based upon the detailed and otherwise undisclosed information the caller provided to the TIPS Hotlines, which showed that Roderick Nunley and a second individual identified as Michael A. Taylor, B/M, 01/30/67, had been involved in the abduction, rape, and murder of Ann Harrison. The TIPS caller said the victim was abducted from her residence and taken to Nunley's mother's house on the 7400 block of E. 118th Street. The caller stated the suspect gained access to the house by driving Nunley's vehicle into the garage on the backside of the house. He described it as a white, two-story house.

Captain Dean Kelly, Sergeant Steve Rice, Detective Steve Brauninger, Detective Marian McMillan, and Gary Howell of the Regional Crime Lab took part in the first search, along with crime scene staff. Also present were Sergeant Clippinger, Sergeant Pete Edlund, Detective Al DeValkenaere, Detective Dresselhaus, Detective Rog, and Detective McGhee.

Crime Scene Investigators recovered carpet standards from the middle of the carpet area of the recreational room on the east side of the basement, along with a one-inch square of wood paneling, which produced a reaction to luminol testing. CSI also recovered a green-checked shirt from a box sitting along the basement bathroom's east wall. They took carpet sweepings from the recreation room floor and photographed the entire lower level. What appeared to be a piece of burned carpet was retrieved from a fireplace insert positioned along the south wall of the recreation room.

While serving the search warrant on the house where Nunley's mother lived, Detective Matt Rog and Detective Joe Dresselhaus conducted an area canvass of the residences surrounding the house and in the 7400 to 7600 block of East

118th Street to locate witnesses. Unfortunately, no one had information of any value for the case.

✵

The investigators had the community's support, and those with helpful pieces of information were all too happy to share it with detectives.

Roderick Nunley had worked at Baptist Memorial Hospital on June 8, 1989 but failed to return to work after June 21st. Nunley knew he was now a suspect because of the warrant served at his mother's house. The hospital's head of security contacted Detective DeValkenaere at the Homicide Unit on the morning of June 26th. He was aware of Nunley being a suspect in Ann's murder, as he had seen it in the media reports. He provided the detective with the phone and address contact information Nunley gave to the hospital when he applied for a housekeeper's position.

Lee Edwards contacted the hospital security office, where he spoke with Officer Thompson. The detective had confirmed that Nunley was a "no show," had been discharged from his job, and that he had a final paycheck that would be ready for Nunley to pick up at the end of the month. The detective advised Officer Thompson that he requested that hospital payroll forward the check to the security department and place a hold on Roderick Nunley's paycheck. He further stated that if Nunley showed up at the hospital, security officers should hold him for pickup by the KCPD. Officer Thompson noted he would share all the information with the entire security department. Should Nunley show up at the facility, they would put these procedures into place.

On June 26th, a call came from an individual who said that Nunley had just started employment at the House of Lloyd in Grandview, working the 0645 to 1530 shift.

However, no one could ever confirm that Nunley was employed there.

On June 27th, detectives received a telephone call from the credit manager for the Ford Motor Credit Company. He stated that Roderick Nunley was currently behind on his car payments, and the Ford Motor Credit Company was actively trying to locate Nunley. He advised the detectives that their office would contact the Homicide Unit if his company located Nunley.

People who had potentially helpful information supported the police in any way possible. Each tidbit of information, each little detail, helped to turn over another puzzle piece to get closer to bringing the big picture into focus.

CHAPTER 8

Police served another search warrant on the Nunley residence on the 7500 block of East 118th Street on June 21st. The items listed in the search warrant included kitchen knives. Two knives were recovered during this search matching the description provided by Michael Taylor and were sent to the Regional Crime Lab for processing. This time, the responding officers were Crime Scene Investigator Buchanan, the Central Patrol Tactical Response Unit members supervised by Sergeant C. Walker, Detective DeValkenaere, Detective Rog, Detective Jefferson, and Detective Bill McGhee.

When detectives attempted to execute the search warrant, there was no response within the residence. Assuming that the home was unoccupied, investigators gained entry by removing a window from the west bay door of the garage. After entering the garage area, the inner basement door was forced open, allowing access to the upper floor of the residence. Although they did not come to the door, officers discovered that Leslie and Mattie Nunley were home.

Leslie Nunley spoke to the officers about the victim's death and said it did not involve her brother Roderick. She stated it could not have happened because she was at the address on E. 118th on the day the victim turned up missing, and she would have known if something had happened in the basement.

Sergeant Edlund held a post-search conference before leaving the scene and determined that no carpet sweepings had been taken initially, only a carpet standard or sample. Edlund's take on crime scenes was "get it all, get it right, get it the first time." So, he sent the team back in and instructed crime scene investigators to vacuum the carpet and collect the sweepings. They would never know if there was anything relevant to the case if they didn't try once more to get evidence.

As soon as the tactical unit determined Taylor remained incarcerated, McGhee and DeValkenaere drove directly to the prison in Cameron and confronted Michael Taylor with Hurley's information. There was silence after detectives presented all the incriminating details that the tipster gave. Then, Taylor said, "Well, your information is good but..." and the detectives fully expected him to ask for an attorney; instead, he asked to talk to his mother.

Prison officials allowed Taylor to make the call, placing him in a room where he could have privacy but remain in plain view of the detectives. A correctional officer dialed the phone for him, and he told the person on the other end that he wanted to speak with his mother. Taylor said that detectives were at the prison, inquiring about his role in a rape and murder in Kansas City. After several minutes on the phone, he said, "Well, uh, goodbye. I love you." Taylor's mother was not home when he called, so he spoke with his sister, who told him, "She said if I did it, to tell you."

It took no time for Taylor to shift all the blame on Nunley. Nunley was high on a drug binge and could not get an erection but attempted to rape Ann. However, DNA showed that the only person who raped Ann was Michael Taylor.

The prison had a new camcorder with an exterior boom microphone, which they made available to the detectives to record Taylor's confession. The statement was recorded, and Taylor signed a consent form for blood samples and hair samples to be taken for examination by the crime lab.

He would end up confessing twice because, when the tape was checked at Detective DeValkenaere's request before they left, detectives learned the microphone failed to record the audio portion of the video. They discovered that the boom mic disabled the internal microphone and that batteries needed to be placed in the device to allow the record function to work. They took the second confession with the audio functioning correctly. Before the trial began, Detective DeValkenaere had to play both tapes for the court, describing what was transpiring during the first tape with no audio and then allowing the court to view the one with sound.

The problems did not stop with the recording equipment. Taylor agreed to be photographed and provide blood, head, pubic hair samples. Those samples were obtained, logged on a physical evidence inventory report, and delivered to the regional lab for processing, but not before causing the detectives some major angst. The correctional facility's infirmary only had one type of tube for Taylor's blood sample. These came with the wrong stoppers to secure the vial for more than a short time. In addition, long-term storage required refrigeration, so to ensure the sample's viability, the detectives drove back to Kansas City's crime lab, lights flashing and sirens blaring. It was a clarion call that the case had finally been cracked and nothing was stopping the detectives from bringing Ann's killers to justice.

In prison, the rumor mill operates its own form of "social media." It took no time for information to spread through the general population about Taylor. There is an unspoken hierarchy within a prison and rapists—especially those who raped young children—were especially reviled. Because of Taylor's being accused of the rape and murder of a young girl, he needed to be placed in a lockdown area. However, the prison policy was that the warden had to authorize locking down any inmate before the correctional officers could reassign one, and they could not reach the warden. As a result, guards escorted Taylor back to his regular unit. Unfortunately for Taylor, a gang of inmates taught him a lesson, and he was gang-raped so violently that his injuries required surgery and over 80 sutures to correct. They subsequently transferred him to lockdown.

For the first time since her abduction and murder, Ann's killer was experiencing some of what he had subjected his victim to during the hours he held her captive. His terror was only a sampling of what Ann endured, but karma came back around and caught up with Michael Taylor.

CHAPTER 9

On June 23rd, KCPD homicide detectives questioned Taylor at the Western Missouri Correctional Center in Cameron, Missouri, where he was incarcerated on an unrelated conviction. After waiving his Miranda rights, having initially denied any involvement in Ann Harrison's murder, and after being advised of Kareem Hurley's statement, he agreed to give an account of his own.

Taylor gave an oral confession to the crimes as detectives videotaped it. The following is the actual transcript of that videotaped confession. It is exactly as spoken, including errors in grammar, pauses, etc.

DEVALKENAERE: *"This is the videotaped statement of Michael Taylor, in regard to the death Of Ann Harrison, reported on Complaint #89-039985. This Interview is being conducted at the Western Missouri Corrections Center in Cameron, Missouri, on 6-23-89, at 1620 hours. This interview is being conducted by Detective DeValkenaere and Detective McGhee in the presence of Ron Kennedy of the Western Missouri Corrections Center Staff.*

DEVALKENAERE: *Mr. Taylor, Will you state your name, please?*

TAYLOR: *Michael Andy Taylor. (Author's note: His middle name was actually Anthony.)*

DEVALKENAERE: *Your date of birth?*

TAYLOR: *1-30-67.*

DEVALKENAERE: *And your permanent address is?*

TAYLOR: *5439 Garfield (Author's note: This is a current residence. Please respect the privacy of the current residents.)*

DEVALKENAERE: *Are you presently in custody here at the Western Missouri Corrections*

Center?

TAYLOR: *Yes, I am.*

DEVALKENAERE: *For what?*

TAYLOR: *Burglary, Tampering.*

DEVALKENAERE: *Returning your attention to this Miranda Waiver Form, were you advised of your rights via this form?*

TAYLOR: *Yes, I was.*

DEVALKENAERE: *Is this your signature on the form?*

TAYLOR: *Yes, it is.*

DEVALKENAERE: *Stating that you understood your rights...*

TAYLOR: *Yea'...*

DEVALKENAERE: *With that in mind, would you state to me, in your own words, the events as you know them leading up to the death of Ann Harrison?*

TAYLOR: *What you mean? ....what happened ...okay, uh ...me and Roger Nunley, we was you know, riding around. We had just got through doing ... doing some, you know, taking some T-tops and stuff like that you dig, and sold them to Doyle, this dude named Doyle, down on Truman, Truman, Truman Road ... it's in Independence, a body shop named Fletch's Body Shop. On our way coming back from that I was driving, you know ... we passed this girl you know, I guess this broad named Ann and Roger told me to stop. So I stopped, and I backed back ... he told me to back ... so I backed back. Then he got out of the car and started talking to her, you know, and then he sort of dropped his shoulder and you know rushed her off into the car. You know. hitting her about right here.*

DEVALKENAERE: *So, he picked her up on his shoulder.*

TAYLOR: *Right, and sort of Like... you know, a tackle... tackled her on into the car. She did, you know, she'd sort of like a flip in the head, ended up in the, you know ... in the passenger side on the floor and her feet was up on the driver's side, you know, on the seat*

*kicking at me . She was doing some
kicking and some screaming and you
know sort of like when you're on
crack and... uh, you know, Roger, you
know was telling her, you know, be...
' be quiet, be quiet, we're not going
to do nothing" to her, and she kept on
screaming and screaming and stuff .
You know saying all kinds of stuff and
he grabbed a screwdriver and put it
at her ribs ...down here somewhere,
and he told her if she did not be quiet
he was going to stick her with it. So
she'd be quiet, you know, and uh...
he told me to drive to his momma's
house. So I drove to his momma' s
house, and you know, I backed the
car up into the garage, and uh, you
know we parked it right there, you
know and uh... I got out the car. We
both got out the car, you know, he got
the girl, he go upstairs... he told me
to go on and take the girl to this little
den like room in their basement...
and uh... you know, I took her in
there and set her down... you know,
and then he came back downstairs.*

DEVALKENAERE: Was she tied up or blindfolded at this
point?

TAYLOR: Yes, she, yes, she's tied up, she had
some cable wire, that's when the
cable wire was put on her.

DEVALKENAERE: When you got to Roger's momma's
house...

TAYLOR:	*Yeah, you know, sock was put around her face in the car.*
DEVALKENAERE:	*Where, where the sock come from?*
TAYLOR:	*Off his, off his foot.*
DEVALKENAERE:	*Roger's foot?*
TAYLOR:	*(no verbal answer)*
DEVALKENAERE:	*Then what happened?*
TAYLOR:	*Then you know... he started taking her clothes off, she doing like this, you know. You know, so I asked him what we going to do to her, you know. He kept on taking her clothes off, you know, telling her to be quiet, be quiet, you know, she was like started crying, and you know, sort of being quiet though, you know, trying to hold her, hold her, from being loud and then maybe he can do something to her, you know, so she can, you know, sort of being cool. And, uh... he took all her clothes off. Then he started having intercourse with her and got... he told her to get on her back, you know. He started having intercourse with her, you know... and I was sitting, you know, sort of like in a block, you know... listening and, you know, sort of tripping out, you know. I said, damn, you dig... and when he got through he came back. He asked me, you knows why don't you go ahead (inaudible), dog ....*

and I sort of said, "Nah. " You know, he said, "Go ahead, man", you know, like that, and I went ahead and went in there too. you know ... and we started having intercourse... I got off in into it... and, but I really did not get off into it, you know, sort of like mixed up, you know, saying "Damn, this fucked up", you know, and I just can' t (inaudible) you know. I just came up out of it you know, I said "Nah, man" you know, "That's not what's happening."

DEVALKENAERE: So you didn't finish?

TAYLOR: No, I didn't finish.

MCGHEE: Can you describe this room that you were in?

TAYLOR: The who? who?

MCGHEE: The room.

TAYLOR: The room is, is carpeted room, you know, with a board kind of like boards where they're doing some remodeling in there, you know, we can of involved having two windows, basement windows.

DEVALKENAERE: You earlier, this is the second statement, because the first statement, the sound didn't work. Earlier in the first statement you told us that, uh... you described the house for us, can you describe it again?

TAYLOR: *Yes, I faced it, faced north, north like going north.*

DEVALKENAERE: *What street is it on?*

TAYLOR: *I don't know the street; it's on 118th.*

DEVALKENAERE: *118th...*

TAYLOR: *... and Terrace.*

DEVALKENAERE: *Okay, it faces north, so it sets on the south side of the street.*

TAYLOR: *Right.*

DEVALKENAERE: *What color is it?*

TAYLOR: *I don't know that. I think it's like pink*

and white.

DEVALKENAERE: *Pink and white...*

TAYLOR: *Yes.*

DEVALKENAERE: *Okay... you mentioned earlier that there was a garage that went to the basement?*

TAYLOR: *Yeah.*

DEVALKENAERE: *What side of the house is that on?*

TAYLOR: *It's on the left-hand side, facing east. When you're going north it's on the left -hand side.*

DEVALKENAERE: *Facing, the house sets north and it's on the...*

TAYLOR: *Right, when you go in the garage, going in the garage, going north...*

DEVALKENAERE: but then, okay; so as you're going
                   in...

TAYLOR: It's on the east side.

DEVALKENAERE: The east side? The garage door
                   actually faces south...

TAYLOR: The garage door faces north... you
                   standing like this...

DEVALKENAERE:... but, the...

TAYLOR: ... garage door...

DEVALKENAERE:... but... the locked the garage door on
               the south side of the house.

TAYLOR: Right.

DEVALKENAERE: Okay. so you drew this drawing, this
                   is coming from the garage, east.

TAYLOR: Coming in, inside, it's coming
                   inside the garage. This is the little
                   bathroom.

DEVALKENAERE: There's a small bathroom here?

TAYLOR: Small bathroom, yeah.

DEVALKENAERE: What is the "X" with the circle on
                   the end?

TAYLOR: Where Ann was.

DEVALKENAERE: On the floor... is that where she was
                   raped?

TAYLOR: That's where it started at.

DEVALKENAERE: Where did it end up at?

TAYLOR:	*That's where it ended.*
DEVALKENAERE:	*Okay, so that, this X With the circle around it, that's where she was raped? The general area.*
MCGHEE:	*Then what happened?*
TAYLOR:	*Then you know, he untied her hands, you know, let her put her clothes back on. She was sort, you know, she was crying still, you know. We sitting there, looking at her, you know, he's sitting there looking at her, you dig, and she's putting her clothes back on, she, you know, telling us that you know, you gonna call her people, gonna call her people, and he said, "Yeah." You know, he let... before he tie her hands, he let her tie her hands, you know, you know, write her number down and address, you know, then to get in touch with her people.*
DEVALKENAERE:	*Why, did she want him to do that?*
TAYLOR:	*She was telling that, you know, they got some money and some of them would... stuff like that.*
DEVALKENAERE:	*Why, why would she say something like that?*
TAYLOR:	*I guess maybe thinking that, you know, hoping her parents could do something.*
DEVALKENAERE:	*She thought, you thought that?*

TAYLOR: Yeah.

MCGHEE: And then what happened?

TAYLOR: And, you know, we brought her back in, we both was leading her, you know, because you know, we had put that blind back on her. The sock, the sock back on her She was tied up, then we led her back on into the garage, and you know, helped her into the trunk. And she sort of like didn't want to get in the trunk, it seems like, you know, I guess sort of, you know, knowing what, you know, tripping off ; man they put me in the trunk, they gonna kill me, you know, and she started acting, you know, crying again, you know. You know, telling, saying how she won't get in the trunk. Roger told her to get in the trunk, so you won't be seen in the car. So, she got in the trunk, you know, and, uh ...

MCGHEE: Did she struggle?

TAYLOR: No, she didn't struggle before getting in the trunk I guess she went with that. You know, she went on with that, you know, and uh... she got on in the trunk. We helped her, both in the trunk, put one leg in and the other leg in. She laid back on both of us, you know, just laid on in there... Roger was telling me to watch her. I was standing there watching and he went upstairs and got two knives A *big one and a little one. And when he came downstairs, you know, he said, "Stick her" I said, ' 'Nah.*

MCGHEE: *He gave you one of the knives?*

TAYLOR: *Yeah, he gave me one of the knives.*

MCGHEE: *Which one did he give you?*

TAYLOR: *He gave me the small knife. (inaudible)*

DEVALKENAERE: *You drew, earlier you drew this drawing of a knife. This larger one being a butcher knife, that, that Roger had and the smaller one being a serrated knife that you had.*

TAYLOR: *Yeah.*

DEVALKENAERE: *Okay, is this what you drew?*

TAYLOR: *Yes, it is.*

DEVALKENAERE: *Is, is this your signature?*

TAYLOR: *Yes, it is.*

DEVALKENAERE: *Then what happened?*

TAYLOR: *Then, you know, Roger asked me to stick her, you know, I said, you know. I said, "Nah.' You know, she said some crazy things you know, cause you 're scared...*

DEVALKENAERE: *And at this point she is in the trunk. This is another drawing, this is a drawing of the car ... uh ... this is Ann here?*

TAYLOR:	*Yes.*
DEVALKENAERE	*What is this X?*
TAYLOR:	*This is, uh. Roger.*
DEVALKENAERE:	*This where Roger was standing?*
TAYLOR:	*Where Roger was standing.*
DEVALKENAERE:	*Where would that be?*
TAYLOR:	*On the, uh... driver's side in the back of the car.*
DEVALKENAERE:	*By the trunk... what is this small line here?*
TAYLOR:	*That's me.*
DEVALKENAERE: happened?	*That's where you're at... what*
TAYLOR:	*And he reached, he reached in the car and grabbed her by the head.*
DEVALKENAERE:	*With which hand?*
TAYLOR:	*With his...*
DEVALKENAERE:	*Grabbed her hair with...*
TAYLOR:	*His left hand ...*
DEVALKENAERE:	*... with his left hand?*
TAYLOR:	*He just sort of like, he didn't grab her hair, he just, you know, grabbed her, You know. You know, went across her throat, it didn't cut, you know, she sort of balled up like that...*

DEVALKENAERE:	*Why didn't it cut?*
TAYLOR:	*It was a dull knife.*
DEVALKENAERE;	*The knife was dull?*
TAYLOR:	*Uh—huh.*
DEVALKENAERE:	*Then what happened?*
TAYLOR:	*Then, you know, he grabbed her, you know, and he went across again and he stopped, he just stuck it in there, you know, just held it there, you know... and, you know, blood, all that blood started coming out and he let it, you know... in there.*
DEVALKENAERE:	*About how much of the knife?*
TAYLOR:	*Just...*
DEVALKENAERE:	*So almost all of the blade?*
TAYLOR:	*It went through.*
DEVALKENAERE:	*It went all the way through her neck?*
TAYLOR:	*Yeah.*
MCGHEE:	*What did he do?*
TAYLOR:	*Then... um... he was babbling, you know, saying crazy things, and stuff like that to me...*
DEVALKENAERE:	*Did he just stab her once?*
TAYLOR:	*He stabbed her a couple times. He stabbed her in the neck, he stabbed her by her heart, and just, you know,*

I'm telling him was she still breathing. You know, he hit her, you know, in the heart, you know, telling me, "Man, stick her. Man, stick her." You know, I guess so that started it, you know, we both in this together. You know, so I stuck her, two or three times, probably four, you know, I stuck 'em in the stomach down here, you know, backed up on away from the car, you dig, so... like tripping out, you know, and uh... he, he had left the trunk open, you know, until she, you know, just you know, didn't wasn't moving no more, wasn't breathing. You know and then I stayed and watched it, you know... her eyes rolled up in her head, and she was sort of like trying to catch her, her breath. She couldn't breathe, you know. And... uh... and he asked me, you know, thought she was dead. He asked me to drive the car and I told him "Nah. You know, we got into an argument about that you know, telling me I'm scared, this, that and the other, you know... pussy this, pussy that... but uh... you know, told him, I'm still not driving the car you know. And. Uh... -he told me to drive his car, so I drove his car, you know.

DEVALKENAERE: *What kind of car was it?*

TAYLOR: *Buick Electra.*

DEVALKENAERE: *What color?*

TAYLOR:	Gold.
DEVALKENAERE:	Is this the car he was arrested for stealing that he had tried to retag?
TAYLOR:	Yes, it is. And, you know, I went outside, got in the car and then, you know, he pulled the Monte Carlo out of the driveway out to the front you know, and he came out of the house, you know... on behind, behind me...
KENNEDY:	Wait a minute. Go.
DEVALKENAERE:	Apparently, we've had video difficulties, battery on the guy's video camera failed. We are now on AC power. This is a video tape of uh... Michael Taylor, being conducted at the Western Missouri Correctional Institute, or Correction Center, on 6—23—89, at 1740 hours. Have you been advised of your rights Michael?
TAYLOR:	Yes, I have.
DEVALKENAERE:	Keeping those in mind, do you still want to talk with us?
TAYLOR:	Yes, I do.
DEVALKENAERE:	Uh... when the tape ended or stopped you were talking about, uh...you had just left...
TAYLOR:	Roger's mother's.
DEVALKENAERE:	Roger's mother's house. Okay, go on from there...

TAYLOR: We left Roger's mother's house, and he was trailing me, you know, and prior to the time before we left he said he was going to blink his lights wherever he was gonna dump the car at. But we was going along the road, and got to some lights and we turned right. You know, and he followed me. Went down two blocks and made a left, and went on to, to, uh... the residential area, you know... he do his lights you know, andturned down left, going left and I went a block extra and, you know, I picked him up, he was on, coming through a park, and I went back on that busy street and turned off the busy street and there was a park right there, I seen him walking through the park. And he got in the car and stuff like that, you know, and went on back to his crib.

DEVALKENAERE: So prior to leaving his mother's house, you had arranged for uh... he'd be following you and he would signal when he was going to turn off 'cause he flashed his lights, and then you would turn on the next street after that?

TAYLOR: Around the block.

DEVALKENAERE: Okay. Come around the block cause he didn't want his car being seen. When you picked him up. What happened when you got back to his mother's house?

TAYLOR: When he got rid of you know, the cable wire, I don't what he did, what he did with that...

DEVALKENAERE: And that's what the, the cable wires is what she was tied up.

TAYLOR: The sock that was around her eyes had blood on it and he flushed that in the toilet.

DEVALKENAERE: Flushed the sock with the blood on it that was around her eyes, down the toilet?

TAYLOR: Yeah.

DEVALKENAERE: Was the cable bloody?

TAYLOR: Yeah, to the best of my knowledge it was, it was around her hands, she was holding them like that.

DEVALKENAERE: Okay, earlier you said something about you didn't see him get rid of the knives, but...

TAYLOR: I don't know, I don't have the slightest idea what he...

DEVALKENAERE: But he asked you to get rid of them because he didn't want his mom to cook with them...

TAYLOR: Right.

DEVALKENAERE: *You also said something about later on he would have a knife in his hand and make some kind of statement.*

TAYLOR: *We would be eating, you know, he would have a knife in his hand, he said, "Here, man, here's the knife" you knows the knife that killed Ann, you know, this bull—chicken shit, you know.*

DEVALKENAERE: *Earlier in the evening, or the night before you picked up Ann, you said that you were driving around stealing T-tops from the cars? Where was that at?*

TAYLOR: *It was in the Raytown area.*

MCGHEE: *Raytown area... what car were you in then?*

TAYLOR: *The SS.*

DEVALKENAERE: *The Monte Carlo SS, the same car you picked up Ann in?*

TAYLOR: *Sure is.*

DEVALKENAERE: *Same car she was found in... is this a photograph of that car?*

TAYLOR: *Yeah.*

MCGHEE: *Do you know who owns that car?*

TAYLOR: *No, I don't.*

MCGHEE: *Do you know where that car came from?*

TAYLOR: *No, I don't, it was just parked in a driveway, and it was parked against the garage. That day that me and him drove around in it.*

DEVALKENAERE: *But when you, but earlier when you were stealing the T-tops, did anything happen?*

TAYLOR: *Well, one instance, we got chased by the police.*

DEVALKENAERE: *What happened during that instance?*

TAYLOR: *We was coming from Raytown and we were in Raytown... we was on the highway and, uh... police got behind us, you know, I was in the backseat, you know, rearranging the T—tops, 'cause they were clashing together, you know and I didn't want them to break. You know, so I put some towels in between them, you know, to give a little cushion, you know. The police got behind us, you know, he said me "police behind us", and I ducked, you know, and the police turned on his lights, and you know, uh... well, you know started going real fast and I climbed back over the front seat, you know, just in cases you know, get stopped somewhere and I can jump out. You know, we lost the police.*

DEVALKENAERE: *Do you know where you lost them at?*

TAYLOR: *On the highway... we left them.*

MCGHEE: During the time that you were with Roderick had anything... anything to drink alcoholic?

TAYLOR: We smoked some weed. Marijuana and some coolers.

DEVALKENAERE: Wine coolers?

TAYLOR: Yeah.

MCGHEE: How much had you smoked during that time?

TAYLOR: We smoked a lot of weed.

MCGHEE: From that time that you were chased by the policemen, up until the time that you picked up Ann Harrison?

TAYLOR: Yes.

MCGHEE: How much do you think you had?

TAYLOR: Maybe five or six joints.

MCGHEE: A piece?

TAYLOR: No, together.

MCGHEE: Five or six joints together?

TAYLOR: Yes.

MCGHEE: And how many wine coolers have you had?

TAYLOR: A whole pack. Four, come four in a pack.

MCGHEE:	*As I understand It, you were stealing T-tops in the south part of town. Where did you take those to?*
TAYLOR:	*Down to uh... Truman Road in Independence, to uh... a dude name Doyle. I don't know...*
DEVALKENAERE:	*Doug?*
TAYLOR:	*Doyle... D-o-y-l-e*
DEVALKENAERE:	*Doyle...*
TAYLOR:	*Yeah, then Doyle, be at Fletch's Body Shop.*
DEVALKENAERE:	*That's F-l-e-t-c-h?*
TAYLOR:	*Yeah.*
MCGHEE:	*Where's that at?*
TAYLOR:	*Down on Truman Road in Independence.*
MCGHEE:	*Independence, Missouri... and what time of day was that?*
TAYLOR:	*It was in the evening time. They open at 9:00.*
MCGHEE:	*Was that the day that Ann Harrison was picked up or the day before?*
TAYLOR:	*Before.*
DEVALKENAERE:	*Was that before or after you got chased by the police?*
TAYLOR:	*It was before.*

DEVALKENAERE:	Before you got chased, chased by policemen, so... when did you get the T-tops in that you had in the car when you got chased by the police?
TAYLOR:	Nah, they wasn't (inaudible) it was two sets in there and after we got done being chased by the police we, you know, we shot down into the city from Raytown, he said, "Don't trip", you know, Kansas and Raytown don't got, you know, a stipulation...
DEVALKENAERE;	Okay .
TAYLOR:	(inaudible)
MCGHEE:	(inaudible) stay at the body shop?
DEVALKENAERE:	Yeah? the same one?
TAYLOR:	Yeah, Fletch Body Shop.
DEVALKENAERE;	Okay, so the police chased you sometime after midnight before, before the sun comes up.
TAYLOR:	Yeah.
DEVALKENAERE:	Okay, prior to that you said that you don't know where the car was stolen from. You told me that...
TAYLOR:	He was already using it...
DEVALKENAERE:	When you got down to his mother's house...
TAYLOR:	In his car, the car was already in the garage...

DEVALKENAERE: And this was the evening before Ann was picked up?

MCGHEE: Had you ever been with Roger when he stole a car?

TAYLOR: Yes, I have.

MCGHEE: How does he break into them?

TAYLOR: Well, either he can do it or I can do it, you know. There's a keyhole, the hole you put the key in it, you know, pry that off the frame of the car.

MCGHEE: With what?

TAYLOR: With a screwdriver. So, there'll be no tool. Just jar it off a little bit, and turn and pop the door open.

DEVALKENAERE: Pop the door open.

TAYLOR: And you pop, pop the door, then you tilt it.

MCGHEE: After you get the door open...

TAYLOR: Tilt it...

DEVALKENAERE: Tilt it, means...

TAYLOR: You break the steering column.

MCGHEE: What items are removed from the cars?

TAYLOR: Cassettes.

MCGHEE: Cassette stereos, radios?

TAYLOR: The dome light be taken cause when you open the doors the light pops on.

MCGHEE: Were there any other items taken out of the car for any reason?

TAYLOR: Cassettes, you know.

DEVALKENAERE: You mentioned the ash tray.

TAYLOR: The ashtray we take 'cause fingerprints might have been put on it, or you know, fingerprints on cigarettes butts.

MCGHEE: So, you can just toss it out the window. Was the ashtray that was in the Monte Carlo still in there when you parked it, or was it taken out?

TAYLOR: I don't know. It's uh... I'm pretty sure it was gone, but, you know, but I checked and it was already gone.

MCGHEE: The reason why that would have been thrown out just to dispose of any evidence that may have been in it, is that correct?

DEVALKENAERE: In prior, in prior instances where you went in, uh... you and Roger had stolen cars, one of, one of, one of you would of thrown it out?

TAYLOR: Yeah, thrown it out.

DEVALKENAERE: I'm showing you six photographs of black males. I realize number two is a picture of you, is there anyone else *in this photograph spread that you recognize?*

TAYLOR: *Number five and number four.*

DEVALKENAERE: *Who is number five?*

TAYLOR: *Roger Nunley.*

DEVALKENAERE: *For the record, that's a picture of Roderick Nunley, a black male, 3-10-65. Are these your initials?*

TAYLOR: *Yes, it is.*

DEVALKENAERE: *On the back of the photograph ... Uh ... number four is who?*

TAYLOR: *A guy I did some time with.*

DEVALKENAERE: *Is he related to this offense?*

TAYLOR: *No, he's not.*

MCGHEE: *Before this date, did you have any knowledge of Ann Harrison... did you know her... did Roger that you know of?*

TAYLOR: *(no verbal answer)*

MCGHEE: *Did you have any idea when you stopped Harrison... did you know what Roger's actions were going to be?*

TAYLOR: *No, I didn't.*

DEVALKENAERE: *I'm showing you, uh... Consent to Search Form, uh... signed by you, is that your signature?*

TAYLOR: Yes, it is.

DEVALKENAERE: Did you sign it of your own free will?

TAYLOR: Yes, I did.

DEVALKENAERE: Have you been offered anything to make this tape?

TAYLOR: No, I haven't.

MCGHEE: Anything to add?

TAYLOR: Yeah, you know, uh... I feel, you know, bad, you know, (inaudible) I didn't want it to happen, you, I didn't. you know, I didn't want to do; I didn't think it was going to happen like it did, (inaudible), you know was all for letting her go, you know, he, you know wanted to kill hers just so she wouldn't be pointing at him, you know. Saying he did it to her, pointing at his face up in court (inaudible) she didn't want to see him, he didn't want to see her pointing at him in court, telling them that he raped her, you know.

MCGHEE: Why did he want you to stab her?

TAYLOR: Just 'cause, you know 'cause I was with him and he told me to stab her, you know... being as we're partners or whatever you know.

DEVALKENAERE: You mentioned earlier that you've been having nightmares.

TAYLOR:	*That, when I was in the county jail, you know, I was (inaudible) and had my weekend (inaudible), and you know I had unhappy nightmares about that, you know, that's why I'm getting my say here, you know. Of my own free will.*
DEVALKENAERE:	*This concludes the videotaped statement of Michael Taylor on June 23, 1989, at 1750 hours.*

Sergeant Cole instructed Detective William R. Martin to issue the following pickup order for Roderick Nunley after they got Taylor's confession.

"Issue pickup on 89-039985 for homicide, for Nunley, Roderick black male, 3/10/65, moniker "little Roger' FBI#832471AA8

SSN XXX-XX-XXXX, 5'5'", 130 lbs., black hair, brown eyes, small build, dangerous and will resist arrest, KCPD #160029, 1914 E 55th Street, mother lives at 7405 E 118th street, KCMO drives a Buick four-door, brown, Missouri 1989 RRB674, Autho. Detective W. Martin Capers, DA, EOMR."

CHAPTER 10

On June 24th at 2:00 p.m., detectives went to an address on the 1900 block of East 55th Street to locate Roderick Nunley when they contacted Leslie Nunley again.

At that point, Ms. Nunley admitted she had lied to the detectives on June 21st to protect her brother Roderick. Ms. Nunley declined to say anything further and refused to accompany the detectives to the Homicide Unit so that they could take a formal statement.

A warrant for arrest was issued on June 24, 1989, and Judge George Aylward signed it, setting the secured bond amount of $125,000. It charged Roderick Nunley with one count of murder in the first degree, one count of armed criminal action, one count of kidnapping, and one count of rape as a Class A felony.

The 160-squad as it was known in department nomenclature, kept Nunley's mother's home under surveillance from June 24th at 1:30 p.m. until 3:00 a.m. the following day to apprehend Roderick Nunley. However, they could not capture him as he never came or went from home. By then, he was once again staying near Troost Lake, a high crime area in the central part of the city.

Locating Nunley in Kansas City was not as successful as finding his incarcerated accomplice. He had successfully eluded tactical officers in car chases until they finally caught him in July 1989.

On July 8, 1989, a caller contacted the 9-1-1 dispatcher at 1836 hours to report a sighting of Roderick Nunley near Troost Lake. The city would dredge the lake periodically, locating stolen cars, various stolen items, guns, and even bodies. The lake was between the Paseo to the west, Vine Street to the east, 27th Street to the north, and Troost Lake Drive to the south. Adjacent is an area known as Troost Lake Park, 3036 the Paseo, notorious for assaults, narcotic transactions, and drug-related shootings.

Kansas City constructed the park and the spring-fed lake as part of a city beautification project in 1899 as the city expanded southward. However, during the desegregation of schools in the 1950s, Troost Avenue became the racial dividing line for the city. As a result, when Kansas City redistributed funding for the development of Ward Parkway, monies for the upkeep of the Paseo dwindled, and the area declined rapidly.

Officers Rick Smith, Pat Delaney, and Sergeant Asa Steen were dispatched to the area to locate Nunley. Sergeant Steen spotted Nunley and directed Officer Delaney to his location. Delaney approached Nunley to question him, and Nunley took off on foot. He ran eastbound between houses in the area. Sergeant Steen and the two officers caught up with Nunley at 28th and Highland, where Nunley identified himself and was taken into custody on the outstanding Jackson County Warrant CR893323. They transported him to police headquarters for booking and interrogation.

When Nunley was questioned, detectives presented him with the information that Taylor provided in his confession. Nunley insisted Taylor would never give him up to the police and said, "If he confessed, show me the video."

Detectives brought a 13" TV/VCR into the room and played the tape for Nunley. He sat motionless, his face no farther than 18" from the screen, watching as his accomplice not only gave him up but placed the blame on Nunley.

"That's bullshit. I'll tell you what really happened" was Nunley's reaction to what he saw. The interrogation lasted approximately 90 minutes, and nothing of significance surfaced that differed from Taylor's statement except who took the lead in Ann's abduction, rape, and murder. Both suspects confirmed Ann was murdered in the trunk of the vehicle they had stolen. Neither denied stabbing Ann, but each blamed the other for initiating the decision to kill her.

For Detective DeValkenaere, who had been to the crime scene, helped move the victim's body, and observed her autopsy, this proved to be the most personally painful part of the investigation. It was beyond the pale to sit there listening to Nunley describe how—after being violently raped—Ann was made to crawl to the garage on her hands and knees, where he and Taylor forced her into the vehicle's trunk. The young girl had been kidnapped, psychologically tortured, physically assaulted, and then required to crawl like an animal to the place where they executed her. Nunley casually related it all.

The dedicated detective who doggedly worked this case would later say that he had to move his hands from a folded position on the table in the interrogation room and place them underneath him to keep from lunging across the table at Nunley. "For the first time in my career, I truly wanted to do that."

Before being interviewed, Nunley read his rights and was presented with a Miranda Waiver Form 340 P. D. After being advised of his rights, Nunley stated, "I'm not stupid. I know I have the right to have a lawyer."

Detective DeValkenaere stopped Nunley from saying anything else and asked him if he was requesting a lawyer. Nunley replied, "No," but he refused to sign the Miranda Waiver Form and added he would sign the form when he was ready to talk. He said that, for now, he was just going to listen to what the officers had to say about the known physical evidence and what the second suspect, namely

Michael Taylor, had said about him in Taylor's videotaped statement.

After listening to the detectives and viewing Taylor's statement, Nunley willingly signed the Miranda Waiver Form and said he was ready to tell "what really happened." Nunley was incensed that his so-called friend would provide a statement of any sort to the police, let alone one implicating him. By this time, it was 2130 hours.

The detectives videotaped Nunley's statement as he detailed the events leading to Ann's death. Everything that Nunley stated directly opposed Taylor's confession. It was to be expected; Taylor blamed Nunley, and Nunley pointed the finger at Taylor. For example, Nunley said Taylor had raped the victim and inflicted all the stab wounds to the victim's body, whereas Taylor had claimed that Nunley had raped the victim and inflicted most of the stab wounds on the victim's body.

Not only did Nunley willingly sign the Miranda Waiver, but he also signed a Consent to Search giving the detectives his permission for them to take standards of his head hair, pubic hair, and a sample of his blood. The crime lab would use those samples to compare physical evidence found on the victim's body.

C. S. I. Detective Atchison recovered the hair standards from Nunley at the Homicide Unit. He then transported Nunley to the Truman Medical Center Emergency Room, where a registered nurse on staff at Truman took an evidentiary blood sample. All the samples were recovered by Detective Atchison and taken to the Regional Crime Lab. Finally, officers transported Nunley to the Central Detention Unit and booked him for Jackson County Warrants, charging him with Ann Harrison's murder.

It was now half past midnight on the ninth of July. It had taken sixty days to identify the suspects, with Taylor already behind bars on unrelated charges; it took another eighteen days to locate Nunley and secure him in the Jackson County Jail.

Forensic examination determined that Nunley's hair sample matched hair found on the victim's jacket, and numerous hairs from Taylor were discovered on the victim's clothing and in the passenger side of the stolen Monte Carlo. The sweepings from the basement room in Nunley's mother's house produced head and pubic hairs indistinguishable from Ann Harrison's.

During Nunley's interrogation, he offered information to detectives that not only corroborated what Kareem Hurley had told them, but he implicated Hurley and himself in two additional crimes. He stated he was driving around town in a stolen auto with Hurley about three weeks before when the two men robbed two females during two separate incidents.

Nunley said that the first robbery took place at the Ramada Inn at 71 Highway & Longview Road. According to Nunley, Hurley jumped out of the car and grabbed a young white female's purse, and jumped back into the car, but the female grabbed Hurley in the car and tried to take her purse back. Hurley then punched the woman in the face and knocked her out of the moving vehicle. Detectives confirmed this story by matching it with a robbery report dated June 18, 1989. The person who filed the report was a 19-year-old white female.

The second robbery took place in the parking lot of the Gates Barbeque Restaurant on 40 Highway in Independence, MO. Nunley stated Hurley jumped out of the car and knocked down an elderly female and took her purse as she was trying to get into a truck with an elderly male. The Independence Police Department located a report with the same date as the Kansas City robbery. All the information in that report was consistent with Nunley's story.

What surprised the detectives the most was the next crime that Nunley described. He stated he was present when Kareem Hurley shot and killed a man who went by the moniker "Fat George." Nunley claimed that the crime occurred in a vehicle parked behind Looney's Store at 39th and Prospect. Fat George was allegedly sitting in the car's front seat when Hurley, seated in the back seat, shot Fat George in the back of the head. Nunley said that Hurley only fired once because the gun jammed.

Records in the Homicide Unit revealed an open file naming Hurley and another individual, Carl Branch, Jr., listed as suspects in the death of George C. Taylor, AKA Fat George. However, prosecutors had declined to file charges against them.

In a bit of twisted irony, both Nunley and Hurley were quick to point their trigger fingers, each accusing the other of murdering their friend they so affably referred to as "Fat George."

CHAPTER 11

The following is the transcript from the July 8, 1989, videotaped statement of Roderick Nunley, regarding the homicide of Ann Harrison that occurred on March 22, 1989. As with Taylor's account, it is exactly as spoken, including errors in grammar, pauses, etc.

"Uh,... this interview is being conducted by Detective DeValkenaere and Detective McGhee, on 07/08/89 at 2240 hours, at 1125 Locust, in the Homicide Unit.

DEVALKENAERE: *What is your full name?*

NUNLEY: *Roderick Nunley.*

DEVALKENAERE: *Your address?*

NUNLEY: *1914 East 55th. (*Author's note: This address is a current residence. Please respect the owner's privacy.*)*

DEVALKENAERE: *And your date of birth?*

NUNLEY: *03-10-65.*

DEVALKENAERE: *Have you been advised of your rights?*

NUNLEY: *Yes, I have.*

DEVALKENAERE: *I 'm showing you a Miranda Waiver.*
Are you familiar with this form?

NUNLEY: *Yes.*

DEVALKENAERE: *Is this your signature?*

NUNLEY: *Yes; sir, it is.*

DEVALKENAERE: *You signed it of your own free will?*

NUNLEY: *Yes, I did.*

DEVALKENAERE: *Keeping those rights in mind, would you state in your own words, the events as you know them, leading up to the murder of Ann Harrison?*

NUNLEY: *Yes, I will. Well, the night before, the day before this stuff happened, before the murder, murder occurred, um... me and Michael Taylor, we were out in Grandview, in, in an apartment complex. We was trying to find a ride, so we could get back down, so we could get down in the city. And we, stole, Michael stole, a white Riviera, a white on white Riviera, I think it had burgundy interior. And we went to the, we went to a shopping center like, over on 95th, I think it's about 95th Street, over by where the Old Skateland skating ring used to be. And we stole, um... one T-top off a blackish—grayish colored IROC. It was sitting out in front of a bar. And we stole that, uh... T-top and we left and we rode around out*

*In Grandview for a little while. We
Was trying to find some more T-tops
Where we could get the both of them
off And, uh... after we rode around
for a while we, we realized that the
white car, the white Toronado that
Michael had stole didn't have very
much gas in it.*

DEVALKENAERE: *Was that a Toronado or a Riviera?*

NUNLEY: *I think it was a Riviera. I'm pretty
sure it was a Riviera. And, so we went
back out to the apartment complex
we had, that we had, that Michael
had stole the Riviera from and there
was a red "Z" sitting out there. It was
a red, Z-28 Camaro, sitting out there
and I helped Michael get into the
door by I grabbed the window and
pulled the window back, he stuck his
arm around in the door and unlocked
the door. And, uh... he started taking
the T-tops off. So, I knew that we had,
we had left the car around a couple
of blocks, the white car, and we had
left that one T-top inside of that white
car And, after we done that, when,
okay, while Michael was getting the
T-tops off of the red Z-28, I went over
and I stole, a um ... the blue Monte
Carlo SS, I stole that. And Michael
had got the T-tops off and ran across
the street, we put the T-tops in the
car, and we left. We left from out that
way and we was down in the city. We*

had went over, went down in the city first, came back out, went out to Lee's Summit and the police chased, I was driving. While this is, all this was going on I was driving. And um... Michael said the police was behind us, we was out in Lee's Summit. And so, the police pulled up behind us and turned his lights on and so I took off. I took off, and the police chased us and I lost the police and jumped on this one street and came back over into the city and went, um... we came back down to the city. We cut through Grandview, was south Kansas City, and we, it wasn't Grandview, it was south Kansas City. We went on back down into the city and we was, we was getting high and stuff, and we was hanging around and stuff like that.

DEVALKENAERE: *When you say you were getting high, what were you getting high on?*

NUNLEY: *Well, Michael smokes the pipe, and I was smoking primo rolls. Weed with cigarettes, or, and weed, weed and cocaine, or either cigarette and cocaine, rolled up into a rolling paper. And uh... so, um... the next time we had left from down in the city, well, I think, well morning had started breaking. We had been down in the city messing around all night, so morning had started breaking. So, me and Michael, we, uh... decided to go out in Grandview, over to my mother's house. Well, it's not Grandview, it's actually south Kansas City. So, we was on our way out there, we Cut through the Pepsi Cola Plant, over on 63rd Street and went out 63rd, until we got to Manchester Heights. Got to Manchester, we made a right up into Manchester and went past the apartment complex and we was heading out toward Grandview. Back through those back streets.*

DEVALKENAERE: *Uh-huh.*

NUNLEY: *After that, we ran, okay, well we was both thinking about, well, how we was gonna get some money. We had about three or four sets of T-tops maybe. And, uh... but we wanted some money now. We had to wait till later on for the guy to open up, that was gonna buy these T-tops from us so, uh... we're riding down the street. I'm driving and Michael says, "There go a purse, there go a purse." So, uh... Michael was suppose to get out and snatch that broad's purse. Well, actually her purse was sitting, I think her purse was sitting on the ground. If I remember it right, her purse was sitting on the ground. Anyways, Michael was suppose to get out and get the girl's purse. So, I'm sitting over on the driver's side, like* this, with this hand on the steering wheel, and I leaning over here like this. Well, Mike gets out of the car first, we pull up, and Mike asks her something. So, then, uh... so we pull off and then, uh...

DEVALKENAERE: What did he ask her?

NUNLEY: He asked her, it was an address, it was just an address he just made up in his head.

DEVALKENAERE: What, he was asking her directions?

NUNLEY: Yeah, he was asking her some directions. It was just an address he just made up his, in his head, you know. So he said, "Stop the car, man. Pull back. I 'm gonna go on and get her purse. So I backed the car back up. So he gets out of the car, you know, he is looking down the street, faking it off real good, talking about some directions to her. So, uh... I'm waiting on him to snatch this purse and jump back in the car. So, instead, Mike grabbed the girl and jumped back in the car with the girl. So, uh... we took off, I just heard and you know, just, he jumped in the car, so I took off, you know. Then we started rolling, I looked over and seen he got the girl in the car, so I'm saying ah ... he had the girl in the car and so we, we rode on, so he had her head up under the... up under the *dashboard over on the passenger sides and her legs were slung over by me, on the driver's and I had her legs, like this, and my elbow down on her legs, and I was driving with this hand down... and ah...... so, we went on out to Grandview out south Kansas City to my mother's house, and nobody was there, so we pulled the car up in the backyard... pulled the car up in the backyard and I went and unlocked the basement door. I stuck my hand through the window one of her windows was broken and it was made of ah, like plastic, and ah, so I took the plastic out and stuck my hand In there and unlocked the basement door, and so I got back in the car and backed the car...*

DEVALKENAERE: *This a garage door.*

NUNLEY: *Yes.*

DEVALKENAERE: *In the basement.*

NUNLEY: *Yes... and so I backed the Monte Carlo SS up inside the garage, and ah as we backed... as I backed the car inside there, I went and closed the garage door down. Michael ah. tells me to hand him something, so he can blindfold her. I don't remember exactly what it was, but I think it was a sock, maybe a rag or something like that so I handed this rag to him, so Michael tied.*

DEVALKENAERE: What color was it?

NUNLEY: Ah, as far as I can remember, it was a reddish color, something like that, red or burnt orange, something like that, similar, so, ah... he, Michael blindfolded her... after he blindfolded her, he, he ah... got her out of the car, on he passenger side, over close by the wall, had to crawl on the floor past the basement window, over to the door, where you go into the back room in the basement, down in the rec room, and so, he took her back in there, after we, ah... took her in there and everything... so, ah, Michael had her. I, I made her go sit down. She wasn't, I did not tie her up at this time, so had her to go and sit down. After she went and sat down on this car seat that we have back there, sittin' on top of this wood partition that's made into the floor, from where somebody was going to start remodeling, but anyway, she sat down there. So, Michael got her up, and he had standing over in the middle of the floor, and Michael started taking her clothes off... he started up here and started taking her clothes off and stuff...

MCGHEE: How was she dressed?

NUNLEY: ... ah ...she had on a blouse, some type of shirt and ...

MCGHEE:	What type of jacket?
NUNLEY:	I don't remember if she had a jacket on, I don't remember sir... I do not remember that, but I know she had on a blouse, a bra, and she had on some, I think maybe pink colored pants or something like that.... and anyway, Michael started taking her clothes off, so ah... I'm getting high, right, I'm smoking these Primo joints, so. ah... I'm paranoid, you know, I'm paranoid and so I go on upstairs and stuff, and then ah... Michael called me, tell me... he told me, say "Damn, man this bitch is tight, man, want you give me some grease or some thin' so I went upstairs and I found some TCB grease, I remember that very well, it was some TCB grease because of the smell to it. I remember the smell to it. So, ah I gave Michael this TCB grease and so ah...
DEVALKENAERE:	TCB grease being ah... grease that you put on your hair?
NUNLEY:	Yes sir, some hair grease... so, ah... I gave him the hair grease, so I went on back upstairs, and ah...
DEVALKENAERE:	What did he do with the grease?
NUNLEY:	I guess he used it for a lubricant, you know, to lubricate his self, you know to have intercourse with the girl. So, ah... I went on back upstairs and stuff, so Michael done had sex

with her and everything, so I came back downstairs.. well he had called me again, that's when I came back downstairs. I was upstairs just gettin' high... walking through the house, trippin' off of what's going on. So ah. ... I came back down there Michael had called me, so ah... I came back down there, so he said ah... "Man, I'm through fucking with her, don't you want a get you some?". I said, "Nah man", so he. you know I could just look at him and tell like he wanted me to participate in it... so I got down and I, you know, I act like that I was going to have intercourse with her, but I didn't have intercourse with her and so, after that Michael ah... no, we, we. Let me see what did we do... after that, we took the girl and put the girl into the trunk of the car. We took her and put her in the trunk of the car, and Michael... so, we was standing there for a few minutes, you know, debating what was we going to do, you know what was we going to do, Michael had said that, ' 'Hey man, we, we ought to just let her go man, but how... we can't just let her go because she gonna, you know, I don't want to have nobody to come, standing up In the court room pointing me out, talking about, "Yeah, he's the one who raped me", and so on and so forth... so ah...

MCGHEE:	Was she tied up at this time?
NUNLEY:	Yes sir, she was tied up with a cord that goes to the car stereo amps... the car stereo amps. The amps into the radio...
MCGHEE:	Who tied her up?
NUNLEY:	ah, Michael tied up, no I think I tied her up. I tied her up... I did tie her up...
MCGHEE:	Tie her hands...
NUNLEY:	... yes, sir. I tied her hands like this... I remember. I tied her hands just like that, and so after Michael had... so after we had took her and put her into the trunk of the car, put her in the trunk of the car and then ah... Michael had... okay we was standing there at the trunk of the car debating on hat was we going to do, you know, what was... what are we going do now? And so, ah,... we came to the decision "Just go... he said. "Nah". He said, "We goin' have to kill her." So he said... I I said, 'Man we ain't... we don't have a gun, you know, we ain't got no gun, man to kill her with", so he said, "Go get some... go get a knife... go get me a knife, man go get me a knife", like that, so I went upstairs, and I got two knives. I went upstairs and got two knives, I brought a small steak knife down like this and I brought a big butcher knife

down like that... and I gave Michael the little knife, and I had the big knife, and ah... so, we was standing there looking at each other, so Michael said, "Fuck it", and he just stuck her, and started sticking her .

DEVALKENAERE: *Where?*

NUNLEY: *He was sticking her in her body... ah, in this part of her body, right up in here... down by her heart, up under her breast, somethin' like about right down in there somewhere... and ah... after he stuck her a couple of times, and stuff, then he looked at me and said, ' 'Ah, come on man, we in this shit together," and shit... so I...*

DEVALKENAERE: *How was she in the trunk?*

NUNLEY: *She was laying on her back. She was...*

DEVALKENAERE: *Earlier, you had kind of showed us on the floor...*

NUNLEY: *Well, she was in the trunk, like she was in the trunk like this... Michael had her raised up like this, and he had stuck her like that. He stuck her a couple of times and then ah... he looked at me and then he said, 'Man, what you goin' do, man, come on man, we in this shit together. So, ah. I took the knife that I had and I acted as if I was goin' slice her throat, but the knife was dull and it wouldn't even cut her. So, ah... after that Mike... she still laying in the trunk like this, still laying in the trunk... so she was dying, I could see that she was dying... so Michael stuck her neck, stuck the knife into her neck and screwed the knife like that, pulled her up... and closed the trunk. After he closed the trunk of the car, then we ah... we left out. We stayed there for a little whiles then we. for a few... I guess maybe thirty minutes, then, and we put... we took off in the car, we came out the garage, I closed the garage, and ah... I drove the car around to the front, and we left out of the driveway, and after that I went over to. I don't remember that street name, but its... I think it's, not Food — lane, but ah... it's the way you come from Quik Trip. The street that you come from Quik Trip, at the light...*

DEVALKENAERE: *Longview Road...*

NUNLEY: *Yes; Longview Road... we went across Longview Road, parked the car, I was driving... parked the car got out the car, it was close to a corner... got out the car and we left. We walked back to my mother's house. We went over there, Michael went to sleep, I walked around the corner to my girlfriend's house and got my car, and I got the T-tops, 'cause we had* took the T-tops out and put them in the basement. Took the T-tops and took em down on Truman Road to a guy named Mike Herman, then I sold the T-tops, for some money and some dope.

DEVALKENAERE: When we were talking, prior conducting this statement, you told us that ah... before you took the car and dumped it, that you and Michael got some things together and put 'em in

NUNLEY: yes...

DEVALKENAERE: ... a paper bag...

NUNLEY: We had took the rag, Michael had said, ah... Michael took the rag, had... he had her blindfolded with... that he had her blindfolded with. It was a rag or either a sock, I don't remember very well which one it was, but I remember she was blindfolded with something that I handed him, and he took It and it had blood on it, because he had stabbed her in the neck, and the rag, I guess it fell down and had... it had got blood on it...

DEVALKENAERE: Uh-huh.

NUNLEY: ... and so, we took that, and we put all the stuff in the sack. It was that and it was some little buttons that she had, I'm not sure if she had a jacket on, but I know they was... they was stuck on to her, her blouse ...

DEVALKENAERE: Like?

NUNLEY: like little buttons that you would... with little names and little skits and stuff like that.

DEVALKENAERE: Little sayings. ...

NUNLEY: Yeah, those type of buttons, she had about two or three of those... and he took those and put all that stuff into a sack and...

DEVALKENAERE: Ah... the buttons, the rag from... that she was blindfolded with...

NUNLEY: yes...

DEVALKENAERE: What else?

NUNLEY:...   and the little parts from the car where that we had stole the car at.

DEVALKENAERE: Broke plastic...

NUNLEY: Pieces of broken... broken pieces of plastic, we took that and stuffed that in the sack...

DEVALKENAERE: How about the, the cables she was tied with.

NUNLEY: I don't remember if we put the cable in there... I think we did put the cable in there too.

DEVALKENAERE: And what did you do with that?

NUNLEY: *We eh... later on that night, about 10:30 or something like that... 10:30 or 11:00, we had ah... well after I had came back from Truman Road, I took... I, Michael was still inside the house sleep... so I... we had got up... we had went around to my girlfriend's house for a while, and after we left from around there.... then we came back and that's when we ah... I'm not... I don't remember exactly which way we went, but I think we went down 119th and Mike threw the stuff in the sewer. It was inside a brown paper bag.*

DEVALKENAERE: *On Foodlane around 119th.*

NUNLEY: *It's I think it was on Foodlane, ah... the sewer on Foodlane...*

DEVALKENAERE: *Somewhere between 118th where your mom lives...*

NUNLEY: *Yes...*

DEVALKENAERE: *...and 119th...*

NUNLEY: *...One Of those sewers, Mike threw the stuff in the sewer.*

DEVALKENAERE: *Okay, when ah....earlier you said you had sold the, the T-tops to ... Mike Harmon ...*

NUNLEY: *Mike ...yes, sir...*

DEVALKENAERE: *...wheel place on Truman Road.*

NUNLEY:	*...yes, Payless Tire Store—on, Truman Road.*
DEVALKENAERE:	*PayLess Tire store.*
NUNLEY:	*Yes sir.*
DEVALKENAERE:	*...and you mentioned you sold the radio to. ...*
NUNLEY:	*Ah, I think we sold the radio ... I, I sold the radio to Doyle...*
DEVALKENAERE:	*... And that's Doyle, a man named Doyle at Fletcher's Auto Body...*
NUNLEY:	*yes, with a Ford truck, with primer on it.*
MCGHEE:	*All the T-tops that you sold were full sets...*
NUNLEY:	*Yes...*
MCGHEE:	*You mentioned earlier that there was one car that you tried to get the T-tops off, but you really couldn't get one of them off. ...*
NUNLEY:	*Yes, and we left that inside the brown Riv... the white Riviera.*
MCGHEE:	*The one that you couldn't get off, you left it on the car that you took the other one off of.*
NUNLEY:	*Yes sir.*
DEVALKENAERE:	*Normally, what did you get for a set of T-tops?*

NUNLEY: *A hundred dollars.*

DEVALKENAERE: *A hundred dollars, or...*

NUNLEY: *A hundred dollars or either a sixteenth worth of dope.*

DEVALKENAERE: *Okay ... so, when ah ... how much did you get for the radio?*

NUNLEY: *Ah ... we always sell them about twenty or thirty dollars ...*

DEVALKENAERE: *Twenty ... thirty dollars... and this . . ah ...*

NUNLEY: *Those type were factory radios.*

DEVALKENAERE: *Okay, this Payless Tire Store is right next to Fletcher's Body Shop on Truman Road?*

NUNLEY: *Yes sir.*

DEVALKENAERE: *When we were talking before the statement, you mentioned that ah, you were with Michael on several other occasions, where the two of you were snatching purses.*

NUNLEY: *Yeah, and Michael ...*

DEVALKENAERE: *... and he always said ...*

NUNLEY: *He he's always thinking about doing that type of stuff ...ah, like we, we would be out, we'd go snatch a purse or something, and Michael, he'd say, "Damn man, I want to get ... that's a bad white bitch, right there, man.*

That's a bad white bitch, right there. Man, I'd sure would like to kidnap say me one of these bitches and fuck the shit out of her. He used to say shit like this all the time, but I never did, . you know, we been knowing each other so long, I didn't never think he was serious, though, man, and that day, I just ah ...I found out. I found out something about a friend that I didn't know. I know, he'd, you know, do things, you know, but not nothing like that, and that's bizarre. I know I participated in it, but...

DEVALKENAERE: *Was there anybody else in your mom's house when this happened?*

NUNLEY: *... it happened ... I think. wait a minute, I think my sister was upstairs sleep.*

MCGHEE : *Lesley (sic).*

NUNLEY: *Yes, I think she was upstairs sleep.*

DEVALKENAERE: *You mentioned that Mike made her, made her crawl from the car into the, the, the, like family room in the basement ...*

NUNLEY: *Yeah, because of the basement windows were there, and he didn't want no body to see her go past the basement window.*

DEVALKENAERE: *You made her crawl. ah ... you also talked about asking her ... or either*

Michael or you asked her about some questions about her family, and she ...

NUNLEY: *Yeah Mike, Mike had asked her, did, did her people have any money, and she ... no, he didn't ask, no one asked her that, she was, she, she voluntarily said that. She said, "Well, don't hurt me ... she kept saying, "Don't hurt me, don' t hurt me" ah this is this was after he had raped her, he said, "kept saying, "Don't hurt me", she just kept saying, "Don't hurt me, my people have money, my ... my people will give you some money", cause Michael kept on asking her, "Bitch, you got any money, Bitch you got any money on you, stashed anywhere?" He was saying that to her as he was taking her clothes off and shit ... and, but then she kept on saying that, no, well she ended up saying that her people had some money and stuff, she could get some money from her people ... give her some money ... give us some money, and so Mike said, 'Well, go get a pen" ... he told me to ... we were just ... he was just faking it, so ... just saying, "Go get, get a ink pen and write this down, what she is saying " ...she was blindfolded, she didn't, she couldn't see what I was doing for real, so I faked, like I had got a pen and I asked her, "Now what you say,* what's the, what's the address, the telephone number and name" and stuff like that, and faked like I had wrote it down.

DEVALKENAERE: So, she would believe that you were believe that you were going to try and get ransom for her ...

NUNLEY: So, she wouldn't, you know, get all hysterical, and shit like that.

MCGHEE: You all left the house after you put her in the trunk, after she was dead, you closed the trunk and you left the garage ... come out, north through the driveway, which way did you go from there?

NUNLEY: We went east ...

MCGHEE: On the righthand side?

NUNLEY: Yes sir.

MCGHEE: Where did you go from there?

NUNLEY: Down to the end of that corner, made another right, went back around there we as going to park the car around there, but people was out at that time. ... people was out and about, so we came back around there and past my mother's block, went around to the block before you get to Sycamore, and we made a right there, and went around, went around this little alley-like street, made curve, it curved under down at . the end and we went

	across ah. ...Longview Road, and we parked the car got out and walked back over to my mother's house.
MCGHEE:	*Who was driving the car then?*
NUNLEY:	*I was.*
MCGHEE:	*Was Michael with you?*
NUNLEY:	*Yes, sir.*
MCGHEE:	*Where was he at?*
NUNLEY:	*He was in the passenger seat. We, we was together. We was both in the car, I was doing the driving, and he was in there with me.*
DEVALKENAERE:	*We talked earlier, anytime you are in a stolen car, you mentioned you always drive ...*
NUNLEY:	*I always drive ...*
DEVALKENAERE:	*Why is that?*
NUNLEY:	*Anybody that knows me, and know that I participate in a stolen car act ... they goin' tell you that Roger is not going to be in that car unless he drivin' 'cause I can drive real good, and I don't trust nobody else's driving. I do not trust anybody else's driving.*
DEVALKENAERE:	*So, you feel that you will be able to get away from the police ...*
NUNLEY:	*Right.*

DEVALKENAERE: *About what time was it, you said that you were chased by a police car?*

NUNLEY: *Oh, between 12 and 1:00 0'clock.*

DEVALKENAERE: *In the morning?*

NUNLEY: *No, at night.*

DEVALKENAERE: *Michael with you?*

NUNLEY: *Yes, sir.*

DEVALKENAERE: *After midnight ...*

NUNLEY: *Yes, about 12 or 1:00 0'clock. That's when the police over in Lee's Summit chased us in the blue Monte Carlo SS.*

DEVALKENAERE: *Then you stole that car from the same parking lot that Michael stole the Riviera.*

NUNLEY: *Riviera. Yes sir.*

MCGHEE: *You know what part of town that was?*

NUNLEY: *Yes sir, Grandview.*

DEVALKENAERE: *Do you remember the name of the apartments?*

NUNLEY: *No sir, I don't remember the name of the apartments, 'cause we always come up to them from the back way, and we can never see the name ... they are light duplexes, like ...I remember the apartments are like ... more like duplexes.*

DEVALKENAERE:	Earlier, you signed a Consent to ... Consent to Search. ...
MCGHEE:	I can't find it ...
DEVALKENAERE:	...giving us permission to take standards of your head hair and a sample of your blood, is this the form that you signed?
NUNLEY:	Yes, sir.
DEVALKENAERE:	You signed that of your own free will?
NUNLEY:	Sure did.
DEVALKENAERE:	... and you understand that's to be used to check against the physical evidence we found on her body?
NUNLEY:	Yes.
MCGHEE:	What happened to the knives that you and Mike used?
NUNLEY:	I had put 'em back upstairs in the kitchen.
MCGHEE:	Michael took 'em back upstairs?
NUNLEY:	Yes sir, I took 'em back up there, not Michael, I did. I took 'em back up there and put 'em in the kitchen.
MCGHEE;	And as far as you know that's where they were left?
NUNLEY:	Yes.
MCGHEE:	The weren't disposed of?

DEVALKENAERE:	*You described a larger, like chef knife...*
NUNLEY:	*Yeah, my mother's got a knife that y'all was describing ... it sounded like that was the knife y'all as talking about, and I ...*
DEVALKENAERE:	*About how long was that?*
NUNLEY:	*...want to make it clear that, that ... it's about this long.*
DEVALKENAERE:	*That the blade or is that overall?*
NUNLEY:	*It's got a darkish, blackish looking handle on it ...*
DEVALKENAERE:	*Okay ...*
NUNLEY:	*and at the end it's got a funny shape to -it at the end with a split in the middle . .*
DEVALKENAERE:	*Okay.*
NUNLEY:	*... and that was a knife, it was a small steak knife about that big with brown handle on it ...*
DEVALKENAERE:	*That steak knife, does it have a smooth blade or ...*
NUNLEY:	*No, it has ridges on it ...*
DEVALKENAERE:	*Okay, and the small one is the one that Michael had?*
NUNLEY:	*Yes, sir.*

DEVALKENAERE: *...and the big one is the one you ... tried, tried to cut her throat with, but it wouldn't, cause it was dull ...*

NUNLEY: *Yes.*

DEVALKENAERE: *When you speak of Michael Taylor, you are speaking of the man that you grew up with over ... you been knowing ...*

NUNLEY: *Since I was about, oh, seventeen ...*

DEVALKENAERE: *So, you have known him for how long?*

NUNLEY: *Oh ... I guess about eight or nine years.*

DEVALKENAERE: *Eight or nine years ... and he lived where?*

NUNLEY: *Ah, 54th and Garfield.*

MCGHEE: *54th and Garfield.*

NUNLEY: *Yes.*

DEVALKENAERE: *Is that where his mother Lives?*

NUNLEY: *Yes.*

DEVALKENAERE: *At that time, you lived where?*

NUNLEY: *On 55th. I would just go out to my mother's house, I didn't stay out there, I stayed on 55th.*

DEVALKENAERE: *Why are you giving this statement?*

NUNLEY:	*Because I seen the video statement in from what somebody was saying that Mr. Taylor was saying in the video statement was a bunch of lies, and he had told ... made the statement about this murder case and he had indicated me and putting me in the part that he played, and I didn't ... I don't feel that's right ...*
MCGHEE:	*Was there anybody else involved in this, other than yourself and Michael Taylor?*
NUNLEY:	*No, Sir.*
DEVALKENAERE:	*But you are giving this statement of your own free will?*
NUNLEY:	*Yes, sir, I am.*
DEVALKENAERE:	*Is there anything you want to add to this?*
NUNLEY:	*No sir, not really.*
DEVALKENAERE:	*This concludes the video statement of Roderick Nunley, at 2305 hours, on 7-8-89.*

Finally, on July 8, 1989, Detective Dan Cline canceled the pick-up order for Roderick Nunley, who officers had just booked for Ann Harrison's murder.

CHAPTER 12

On July 28, 1989, a Jackson County grand jury indicted Roderick Nunley and Michael Taylor on first-degree murder, forcible rape, kidnapping, and armed criminal action. But, between the State and the Defense, they would move the case three times before the two could appear before a judge instead of a jury trial for the murder of Ann Harrison.

The first move was to have Judge Levitt of Division 13 removed at the defense attorneys' request; the second reassignment, requested by the State, was to send the case to Division 11 to be heard by Judge Donald L. Mason, who would disqualify himself. Finally, the case was assigned to Division 4 in Judge Alvin Randall's court.

On December 18, 1990, while in custody for Ann's murder, Taylor eloped briefly from Jackson County Jail custody. This escape would be the second time Taylor could slip from the grasp of his jailers. Taylor was being taken to Truman Medical Center for a medical appointment, and police apprehended him nearby after being gone only a short time. Taylor had been planning an escape for months after stealing wire cutters from a maintenance cart left unattended in the jail. The inmate had made a compartment in the sole of his shoe to conceal the tool and used it to cut his leg irons. Then, he slipped out of the handcuffs and broke away from the guards who escorted him to the hospital. He had bolted from the facility but did not get very far before police captured him. The hospital sits less than a mile south of police headquarters.

When officers apprehended him, the coward had the nerve to ask them, "Why didn't you let me go? You know what I'm facing." Why did he not let Ann go when he knew what she faced that day in March after he savaged her, or when they forced her back into that stolen car and stabbed her repeatedly, leaving her alone to die a slow and dreadful death?

✳

At his January 29, 1991 trial, Roderick Nunley stated the original plan was to rob

Ann of her purse. Nunley admitted to abducting and murdering the girl but denied ever raping her. Instead, he stated only Taylor had raped her and that he, Nunley, only pretended to do so to appease Taylor. He said his reasoning for killing Ann was because Taylor said they were both involved and that she could identify them, and so they needed to kill her together.

His logic was bewildering and bizarre. He did not want to go to jail for kidnapping and rape, so he elected to commit murder. Criminals do not think. There is no imagination. There is no ability to project ahead and see the potential consequences of the immediate actions. They live in the moment with no preconceived thoughts on what the aftermath could unfold. The immediate gratification found in Ann's abduction, robbery, and rape spilled over into the actions taken to hide the crime. Criminals are lazy. No work or thought was expended to conceal the evidence or clean up after the crime. The two offenders put more effort into disposing of ashtrays and other items they may have touched in the theft of an automobile. They exhausted the least possible amount of energy required to cover up the ultimate offense.

At Roderick Nunley's plea hearing, he explained his involvement in Ann's murder this way:

Q: Starting with that night, March 21, 1989, who were you with?

A: Michael Taylor.

Q: Ok. Were you two smoking – well, let me ask this. Were you smoking or doing any drugs that night?

A: Yes, we were… .

Q: Ok. At some point that night did you two steal a car?

A: Yes

Q: Ok. Who was driving that car?

A: Me… .

Q: At some point that morning, March 22, 1989, did you two see a girl with a purse?

A: Yes.

Q: And did Michael Taylor tell you that he wanted to snatch that girl's purse?

A: Yes, he did.

Q: Did Michael Taylor then get out of the car and talk with the girl?

A: Yes… .

Q: Did Michael Taylor, after speaking with her, grab her?

A: Yes.

Q: And did he put her in the car?

A: Yes, he did... .

Q: Did you two force her to stay in the car?

A: Yes.

Q: You then drove to somewhere in Grandview, Missouri?

A: Yes... .

Q: You went actually specifically to your mother's house; is that correct?

A: Yes... .

Q: Once you got to that house, you then put the car in the garage; is that right?

A: Yes.

Q: And at some point, did you give Michael Taylor something to blindfold [the girl]?

A: I think I did, yes.

Q: OK. And then at some point he took her out of the car and forced her to crawl down to the basement; is that correct?

A: Yes.

Q: Once the three of you were in the basement, you told her to sit down, did not you (sic)?

A: Yes.

Q: And while you were in the basement, you saw Michael Taylor taking her clothes off, did not you (sic)?

A: Yes.

Q: You then went upstairs?

A: Yes... .

Q: When you came back downstairs, did you see Michael Taylor forcing her to have intercourse with him?

A: Yes... .

Q: At some point did Michael Taylor then ask you to go get him some lubricant?

A: Yes.

Q: And, in fact, did you do that?

A: Yes.

Q: Ok. You never stopped him from committing the rape, did you?

A: No.

Q: After that was over, you two then put her in the trunk of the car you had stolen; is that correct?

A: Yes.

Q: You then tied her up, did not you (sic)?

A: Yes.

Q: And you and Michael Taylor stood there for a while; is that correct?

A: Yes.

Q: And the two of you had a conversation, did not you (sic)?

A: Yes.

Q: Michael Taylor said that he did not want her identifying him in court later on, did not he (sic)?

A: Yes... .

Q: So, at that point you two discussed what to do, did not you (sic)?

A: Yes.

Q: And you two decided to kill her, did not you (sic)?

A: Yes.

Q: You did not have a gun; is that correct?

A: Yes.

Q: So, Michael Taylor suggested using knives.

A: Yes.

Q: And you went upstairs and got two knives from the kitchen.

A: Yes.

Q: And then you took those two knives back down to the garage where Michael Taylor was; is that correct?

A: Yes, I did.

Q: You gave Michael Taylor the little knife, and you took the big knife.

A: Yes.

Q: And Michael Taylor then stabbed her, did not he (sic)?

A: Yes, he did.

Q: And initially he stabbed her in the heart and the chest area a number of times; isn't that correct?

A: Yes.

Q: And Michael Taylor actually told you that he thought you two were in this shit together; do you remember that?

A: Yes.

Q: So, you took your knife, and you also attempted to stab her, did not you (sic)?

A: Yes

Q: Your knife was dull?

A: Yes.

Q: Was Michael Taylor then the one that ended up stabbing her in the throat where you had tried to?

A: Yes.

Q: While you were stabbing her and while Michael Taylor was stabbing her, you never left to go call the police or to get help, did you?

A: No, I did not. ...

Q: You then took both of the knives back upstairs; is that correct?

A: Yes.

Q: And Michael Taylor closed the trunk of the car.

A: Yes, he did.

Q: And you knew that she was going to die, did not you (sic)?

A: Yes.

Q: You drove the car away; is that correct?

A: Yes.

Q: And you parked it in some neighborhood fairly close to the house.

A: Yes.

Q: And on July 8, 1989, you gave a videotaped statement regarding you (sic) participation in this offense, did not you (sic)?

A: Yes... .

Q: And it's your desire, in fact, to plead guilty here today?

A: Yes.

At the plea hearing, Nunley also testified that he knew he was waiving a jury trial and jury sentencing:

Q: Do you understand that by pleading guilty today you're waiving or giving up a certain number of constitutional rights that you would have if you went to trial?

A: Yes.

Q: Do you understand that at that trial you would have the right to a trial by a judge or a jury?

A: Yes... .

Q: Do you understand that if you went to trial and you were found guilty of these charges that you would then start the second phase of the trial, which would be the sentencing phase by the jury; do you understand that?

A: Yes.

Q: By waiving that, you're not going to be sentenced by a jury. Do you understand that?

A: Yes... .

Q: It is still your desire to plead guilty today?

A: Yes, it is.

⁑

After a three-day sentencing hearing, the judge sentenced Nunley to death.

Nunley pleaded guilty to murder in the first degree, along with rape, kidnapping, and armed criminal action. He was informed that he could receive the death penalty but elected to appear before a judge and waive a jury trial. The judge presiding over his case, Alvin C. Randall, was appointed Judge of Division Four of the Sixteenth Judicial Circuit on January 11, 1964. He had never had a death penalty case brought before him in the almost three decades he was on the bench. He had previously handed down only life sentences with no possibility of parole. The attorneys for Ann's killers had done a great deal of research when they began "judge shopping" for the benefit of their clients. The judge scheduled the trial's sentencing phase for March 19, 1991. Roderick Nunley's sentence would be handed down almost two years to the day Ann was murdered.

The Harrisons were present for the testimony, having waited two years for this case to come to trial. It was the start of what would prove to be a recurring nightmare in the daytime, reliving the horrendous details of Ann's abduction and murder. The sentencing was the first time they heard all the gruesome details of what their oldest child had endured on the fateful day that her life intersected with Nunley's and Taylor's. It was a parent's great fear brought to bear. Bob Harrison would later comment on Nunley's "nonchalant" demeanor. "He was up there like he had his driver's license revoked."

Leslie Nunley, the defendant's sister, spoke for the family, affirming that they concurred with the plan to proceed without a jury. She said they thought this was fairer, given that Ann was white and Nunley was black, referring to it as a "racial thing."

Pat Hall, the Jackson County Prosecutor, repeatedly quizzed Nunley in open court, ensuring that Nunley and his attorney understood the law and that there would be no appeal to his election to allow the judge to hear the case solely. However, the years would show that this would not be how the events would play out.

CHAPTER 13

On February 9, 1991, twelve days after Nunley's trial date, Taylor took the stand in Judge Randall's chambers to tell his version of the events that took place, admitting to first-degree murder, rape, kidnapping, and armed criminal action. When Taylor appeared before Judge Randall, the prosecutor questioned him in the same manner that he had done with Nunley. He wanted to document that Taylor understood the implications when he pleaded guilty in 1991. At that hearing, Taylor's defense counsel testified that the State's case against Taylor was "one of the strongest cases [that he] had ever encountered." The strategy would be for Taylor to enter a guilty plea before the judge and focus on the penalty phase to dodge a death sentence. Because of the violence surrounding Ann's abduction, rape, and murder, they decided that the best course of action would be to avoid a jury trial. In the opinion of his attorneys, Randall's history of handing down life sentences was in Taylor's best interest.

The following is an excerpt from Taylor's February 1991 plea hearing transcript:

Q. Do you also understand that if you plead guilty it will be up to the judge to decide the sentence on all charges?

A. Yes.

Q. And as the maximum that you can get on all of these charges, do you understand that the Judge can give you the death sentence?

A. Yes.

Q. If you plead not guilty, do you understand that you have a right to go to trial?

A. Yes.

Q. And if you plead not guilty, there would be a trial.

A. Yes.

Q. Do you understand that the trial would be in front of a jury of twelve people?

A. Yes, I do.

Q. And the twelve people would have to be unanimous in their verdict?

A. Yes.

Q. In other words, all twelve would have to agree.

A. Yes.

Q. The twelve people would have to be convinced beyond a reasonable doubt by the state that you're guilty.

A. Yes.

Q. And that would be on each charge, all four counts; do you understand that?

A. Yes. I do. From the plea hearing transcript at page 13 (emphasis added) (sic):

Q. Michael, do you understand that if you plead guilty there won't be a trial?

A. Yes, I do.

Q. And you, in essence, would be giving up those rights. Do you understand that?

A. Yes, I do.

Q. Sometimes we use the word waive. If you plead guilty, you are waiving the right to a trial by a jury.

A. Yes, I understand.

Q. The right to a trial.

A. Yes, I understand.

From the plea hearing transcript at pages 19–21 (emphasis added) (sic):

Q. Has anyone made any promises to you about how this is going to turn out if you plead guilty?

A. No, they haven't.

Q. You know that if you plead guilty the state is going to ask for a death sentence and the Judge could impose death.

A. Yes, I do.

Q. Now, if you plead guilty, do you understand that all that would be left for the Court to do would be to sentence you?

A. Yes. ....

Q. [D]o you understand, Michael, that there would still be a sentencing hearing where the state will be presenting evidence, and we, on your behalf [,] (sic) will be presenting evidence to the Judge as to what sentence to propose on the murder charge ? (sic)

A. Yes.

Q. And, actually, the Judge can entertain evidence on all of the charges.

A. I understand.

From the plea hearing transcript at page 28 (emphasis added) (sic):

Q. And do you understand that there will be a sentencing proceeding yet to occur in front of the Judge?

A. Yes, I do. From the plea hearing transcript at pages 34–36 (emphasis added) (sic):

Q. Do you understand that ... you might be entitled to two trials, that is, one trial where the jury would decide murder in the first degree and then punishment if they found you guilty of murder in the first degree.... Do you understand that?

A. Yes. ....

Q. No one has guaranteed you what sentence you're going to receive?

A. No.

Q. No promises have been made to you as to what sentence you're going to receive.

A. No, they haven't.

Q. Has anyone told you what sentence you're likely to receive?

A. No, they haven't.

Q. What sentence do you think you're going to receive as to Count I, murder in the first degree?

A. What sentence do I think?

Q. Yes.

A. I do not know.

Q. Do you understand that the Judge might very well sentence you to the death penalty in this case?

A. Yes, I do.

Q. Do you know that by pleading guilty here today that instead of twelve people deciding, there will only be one person deciding, this Judge; do you understand that?

A. Yes, I do.

Q. As to the other counts, the Judge could sentence you to the minimum, or he may very well sentence you to the maximum on each of the other counts charged; do you understand that?

A. Yes. From the plea hearing transcript at pages 38–42 (emphasis added) (sic):

Q. Have your attorneys gone over with you the different stages that occur at a murder in the first-degree trial?

A. Yes. ....

Q. Now, the second phase would be a separate trial in front of the same jury if they do find you guilty of murder in the first degree. Do you understand that?

A. Yes, I do.

Q. It would be like a trial. There would be opening statements. The state would present evidence, and you could present evidence. Do you understand that?

A. Yes, I do.

Q. You would have a right to confront the witnesses, to subpoena witnesses, to subpoena witnesses in. Do you understand that?

A. Yes.

Q. The court would then instruct the jury, the attorneys would argue, and then they would deliberate, the jury would deliberate. Do you understand that?

A. Yes.

Q. During their deliberations, all twelve jurors must find, beyond a reasonable doubt, at least one aggravating circumstance. Do you understand that?

A. Yes.

Q. And if they do not find at least one aggravating circumstance, then they must sentence you to life without parole. Do you understand that?

A. Yes.

Q. Now, the state has filed notice of nine aggravating circumstances, statutory aggravating circumstances. Do you understand that?

A. Yes.

Q. Have you talked about those with your attorney; have you seen those?

A. I'm not real familiar with seeing them, but I have talked with them about them.

Q. When I say that the jury must find at least one, they must find at least one statutory aggravating circumstance. If they do not, it's life without parole. Do you understand that?

A. Yes.

Q. If they do find at least one statutory aggravating circumstance, then they can determine if there are any non-statutory aggravating circumstances. Do you understand that?

A. Yes.

Q. And the state has filed notice, I believe, of [25] or [26] non-statutory aggravating circumstances. Are you aware of that?

A. Yes.

Q. And the jury would determine if the statutory aggravating circumstances non-statutory aggravating circumstances and the evidence in the case, whether they warrant the death penalty. Do you understand that?

A. Yes.

Q. And they must unanimously find that they do warrant the death penalty. Do you understand that?

A. Yes.

Q. And if they do not, then it's life without parole. Do you understand that?

A. Yes, I do.

Q. And then if they find that there are sufficient aggravating circumstances to warrant death, then they must consider whether there are mitigating circumstances. Do you understand that?

A. Yes, I do.

Q. And your attorney has supplied me with notice of five statutory mitigating circumstances that would be presented to the jury; do you understand that?

A. Yes.

Q. And the jury would then consider whether those mitigating circumstances, or the evidence in the case, whether it outweighs the aggravating circumstances. And if they found that the mitigating circumstances outweigh the aggravating circumstances, then they must sentence you to life without parole. Do you understand that?

A. Yes.

Q. And do you understand that when they consider the mitigating circumstances that they do not have to all unanimously find the same mitigating circumstances; do you understand that?

A. Yes.

Q. And do you understand that even if they find that the mitigating circumstances do not outweigh the aggravating circumstances that they still are not obliged to sentence you to death; do you understand that?

A. Yes.

Q. The final decision would rest with the jury. Do you understand that?

A. Yes.

Q. But again in this case it will all be up to one man. Do you understand that?

A. Yes.

Q. Is that what you want?

A. Yes, it is.

✴

Under oath, Taylor insisted he wanted to let the little girl go but was pressured by his companion to stab her. By his own admission, he lacked the moral courage to stand up to his partner in crime, finding it easier to kill an innocent teenager in cold blood than to offend his friend. Taylor spoke of Ann fighting to keep from being pulled into the car, claiming Nunley had done it. He described how she resisted getting into the car's trunk and begged for them to call her parents, insisting that they would pay for her release. For a little girl who had just turned 15 a few weeks before, she had shown courage and logic well beyond her years, traits that her abductors clearly did not possess.

Taylor was 24 years old, and he had already been in the system for years. He had gone to prison and was on parole, serving three years of a six-year sentence for seven different crimes, all to run concurrently. He was not exactly a model prisoner; he had over 40 violations for conduct. Taylor was and had always been a problem. Had he not been released early and, if the courts had required him to serve his entire sentence, perhaps Ann would still be alive. Instead, he did not attempt to change his life, reach out to his family for help, and keep out of trouble.

Taylor's family was in the courtroom that day, sobbing as he told his version of what transpired on that early morning in 1989. The minister of their church spoke to the media and said that the Taylor family was a good one, but said of Michael, "That boy's always been trouble." Taylor's criminal history alone would substantiate the minister's description of his demeanor.

When Pat Hall cross-examined Taylor, he repeated the warning that he had delivered to Roderick Nunley just weeks before. He reiterated that there was to be no appeal to the sentence from Judge Randall, even if Taylor's sentence was the death penalty. Taylor stated in open court that he understood that. However, the future would show that he never really believed it. In the same way he eluded police and twice slipped the grasp of the corrections officers, he was convinced he could escape the executioner.

CHAPTER 14

Set previously by Judge Randall, the sentencing phase of the trials began on March 19, 1991. Nunley's attorney made a plea to the court, telling a story of his early life, abandonment by his father, his use of drugs since 3rd grade. It was hard for the victim's family and friends watching the trial to garner even an iota of sympathy. He had a mother who raised him and a sister who not only defended him but lied to the police on his behalf. He was not homeless. He had access to his mother's home and stayed there occasionally. It was in his mother's house that he and Taylor murdered Ann. He had family and a girlfriend who were in court on his behalf. Nunley was not the only person ever faced with a tough childhood; he more closely fit the profile of a career criminal. Nunley was a car thief, a purse snatcher, and allegedly a murderer of at least one person besides Ann Harrison.

On March 20, Kareem Hurley took the stand to testify about Nunley's involvement in Ann's murder. Hurley had called the TIPS Hotline on June 21, 1989, to tell what he knew and collect the $9,000 reward for information regarding Ann's case. His statements to the hotline substantiated the evidence that police had already gathered. In addition, he had facts surrounding the case that had never been previously disclosed.

In exchange for reductions in charges pending against him for drugs and stealing, Kareem Hurley divulged not only what Nunley had revealed to him about this case but also about another killing that Nunley had bragged about committing. That was also confirmed by law enforcement because they had charged Nunley as one of two individuals who shot a drug dealer named Jonas Dickerson just eight months before Ann's murder. In addition, Hurley confirmed Nunley was also involved in another homicide and provided the location of that alleged crime.

He stated he had known Nunley, who he referred to as Roger, an alias that Nunley used, his entire life. He was a friend, a partner in crime. Hurley described him as paranoid, always watching his surroundings, and said that Nunley was using drugs more frequently in recent years, as though he were trying to block out things that were troubling him. He recounted that Nunley claimed he only attempted to rape Ann to appease Michael Taylor, who insisted that Nunley do so since he (Taylor) had sexually assaulted her. It troubled him those detectives would identify himself and Michael because of pubic hairs they might have left at the scene. Hurley said that Nunley killed Ann because she heard Taylor call him by name, and he was afraid that she could identify him. He told Hurley that he retrieved several knives from his mother's kitchen and started the stabbing.

Kareem Hurley, Nunley's lifelong friend, received his $9,000 besides his sentence reductions. He had satisfied all the requirements for obtaining the monies; now, he could take his pieces of silver and get on with his life, or so it would appear.

After Ann's murder, Nunley continued his practice of getting high, stealing cars and T-Tops, selling the stolen property, buying more drugs, and around and around he'd go. His companion was Kareem Hurley and not Michael Taylor on one of his binges, as Taylor was incarcerated in the Western Missouri Correctional Center in Cameron, Missouri. As was his practice, Roderick Nunley was driving, and Hurley was a passenger as they passed through the parking lot of the Venture Store at the northeast corner of I-70 and Noland Road in Independence, Missouri.

Hurley saw an elderly woman walking through the parking lot and told Nunley to slow down so he could grab her purse. It was a routine that Nunley pulled with whatever companion he was with, only this time, the victim refused to let go and kept clutching her purse. Hurley pulled the woman into the car when Nunley began screaming for Hurley to let it go. He got the bag, and they drove off, but not before the victim fell, breaking her hip.

Nunley was upset and repeatedly called it "de ja boo" instead of déjà vu. When Hurley asked what he was talking about, he responded that it "was just like Annie" and, when pushed, stated that was how Taylor abducted Ann Harrison when all he was supposed to do was take her purse. Nunley told Hurley details that only her killer would know; how he inflicted a wound 2" in diameter in her neck by twisting the serrated knife.

Detectives turned the information over to the Independence Police Department, and they charged Kareem Hurley with robbery. In a strange twist of fate, Hurley spent his $9,000 reward money on a defense attorney in that case.

Ironically, years later, Kareem Hurley would face his own rape and assault convictions—crimes ironically close to the ones he helped get Nunley and Taylor convicted for a decade earlier. Fifteen years after Ann's murder, the tipster who collected the reward for her murder would find himself the focus of the criminal justice system.

In 2003, police arrested Kareem Hurley for armed criminal action, forcible rape, and second-degree assault against a female acquaintance. On December 29, 2003, Hurley invited his victim to his home to eat and spend the evening. Instead, he offered her some crack cocaine, and, as she smoked it, he began stabbing her about the face, head, and abdomen. After stabbing and punching her viciously, Hurley forced her to perform oral sex. He later raped the woman, forcing her to remain in his home until the next day. However, he allowed her to leave the morning after her assault. The victim was found disheveled and stumbling down the street by a friend passing by.

Hurley received a life sentence for forcible rape, armed criminal action, and 2nd-degree assault. Having been sentenced to life in prison for his actions, Hurley remains a permanent guest of the Missouri Correctional Facility in Jefferson City.

CHAPTER 15

At his sentencing hearing on April 25, 1991, Taylor's mother, Linda Taylor, begged the court for mercy for her son. She testified that a few days after the murder, he came home looking disheveled and dirty. She offered to get him some help for his drug use. Instead, he told her, "Mama, only God can help me now," and walked out. Taylor was cognizant of what he had done. However, he was also streetwise enough to know that if he claimed he was innocent and Nunley alone had committed the murder, he could turn on his friend, become the State's witness, and have a chance to avoid what lay before him. He tried it but was unsuccessful in convincing the court that he was merely a bystander to the brutal stabbings that took Ann's life.

Assistant Prosecutor Pat Peters led the last part of the penalty phase for the State against Taylor on April 26, 1991. He appealed to the court, referring to what happened to Ann as "every parent's nightmare." "If this man does not get the death penalty, there shouldn't be a death penalty." His impassioned plea was peppered with details that outlined the brutality that happened to Ann. He described her wounds as "carving" as he referenced the ten gashes that the coroner identified. The child had multiple deep wounds that penetrated her internal organs, resulting in her bleeding to death.

The State's physical evidence included hair matching Taylor's collected from Ann Harrison's body and the passenger side of the Monte Carlo, hair matching Ann's collected from Nunley's basement, and sperm and semen belonging to Taylor found on Ann's clothes and body. An autopsy revealed a lacerated vagina, six stab wounds to Ann's chest, side, and back, which penetrated her heart and lungs, and four stab wounds to her neck.

The medical examiner testified Ann Harrison was alive when all the wounds were inflicted, noting that there was no singular blow inflicted that resulted in immediate death. Although there did not appear to be any defensive wounds showing that she could fight back, the autopsy revealed that Ann was conscious for at least fifteen minutes and alive for about two hours as she slowly bled to death.

In 1991, courts did not permit victim impact statements in Missouri, although many other jurisdictions throughout the United States permitted these to be introduced at the sentencing phase of criminal cases.

It was not until 1994 that the Missouri Supreme Court approved these actions in the State v. Wise. That case permitted the use of victim impact statements to be presented to the jury at the sentencing stage of a capital punishment case.

The Missouri statute, Mo. REV. STAT. § 217.762 (1994) reads:

A victim impact statement shall:

(1) Identify the victim of the offense;

(2) Itemize any economic loss suffered by the victim as a result of the offense;

(3) Identify any physical injury suffered by the victim as a result of the offense, along with its seriousness and permanence;

(4) Describe any change in the victim's personal welfare or familial relationships as a result of the offense;

(5) Identify any request for psychological services initiated by the victim or the victim's family as a result of the offense; and

(6) Contain any other information related to the impact of the offense upon the victim that the court requires.

The Harrisons were denied their only chance to give Ann a voice in court because of rulings that stated that it infringed on the defendants' rights. So, Ann had no rights in court, no voice, no one to beg for her as both Nunley and Taylor did.

On May 4, 1991, Taylor and Nunley each appeared separately in court, with each proceeding taking less than thirty minutes each. Both killers pleaded guilty to first-degree murder, armed criminal action, kidnapping, and forcible rape. Under the advice of counsel, each elected to do so because their respective attorneys believed that Judge Randall was one of the few Missouri judges who might be lenient in sentencing Taylor. They were wrong.

The Harrisons remained stoic as the judge read the verdicts. The judge imposed the death sentence for Ann's murder and consecutive terms of fifty years for armed criminal action, fifteen years for kidnapping, and life for rape. Nunley's girlfriend acted out, trying to run out the courtroom door to leave. She could not exit the locked doors and sobbed at the back of the courtroom. Nunley's illegitimate children would grow up without him in their lives. When it was time for Taylor's sentencing, he knew his fate as he entered the courtroom, his sister crying when the guards escorted him into the room.

※

In October 1991, both Nunley and Taylor appealed their sentences, claiming that the judge was drunk, that the prosecutors were racially biased, and their attorneys were incompetent. It was the beginning of the long road to death. The court had appointed two new defense attorneys to represent Taylor and Nunley. In addition, Judge Randall recused himself from hearing further post-conviction motions because of the accusations lodged against him.

The defense attorneys claimed that the prosecutor's office did not ask for the death penalty because of Ann's vicious attack. Instead, they made it a racial issue, claiming it was because black men murdered a white girl.

The judge assigned Pat Hall and Cramer Anderson Russell to represent the State for these appeals. The State countered the request, citing no facts to support the accusations against either the judge or the prosecutor's office and pointing out the defendants' statements in court transcripts about their levels of satisfaction with their defense attorneys.

Soon, the presiding Circuit Court judge would disqualify all the Jackson County Circuit judges from hearing further arguments about the convictions. Several judges had already recused themselves because of any appearance of bias from having worked with Judge Randall. As presiding judge, he appealed to the Missouri Supreme Court for a magistrate outside the Jackson County area to oversee the case. It seemed reasonable and appropriate for this action so that no further issues could be brought forth. However, these accusations would be brought up repeatedly through the court system as Nunley and Taylor worked to escape what had been a fair and just sentence from the start. As Judge Randall stated in his ruling, "They gambled and lost."

CHAPTER 16

On November 22, 1991, the Missouri Supreme Court appointed Judge Robert H. Dierker from the 22nd Judicial Circuit to handle the appeals. Because Judge Randall was accused of being under the influence of alcohol when he pronounced Taylor's sentence—despite having made the ruling before having a drink at lunch—a special judge was appointed to hear Taylor's post-conviction relief hearing. The allegations that Judge Randall had been drinking during all the trial proceedings would prove unfounded. Three years after Ann's murder, the killers were back in court, attempting to get their sentencing overturned.

According to Taylor's testimony at his guilty plea hearing, which corroborated his videotaped statement and other evidence adduced in the sentencing hearing, Taylor and a companion, Roderick Nunley, spent the night of March 21, 1989, driving a stolen Chevrolet Monte Carlo, stealing "T-tops," smoking marijuana, and drinking wine coolers. During the early morning hours of March 22nd, a Lee's Summit police officer followed them but they lost the police after a high-speed chase on a highway. The officer had to discontinue the pursuit because the suspect vehicle entered Kansas City's limit.

Nunley, a past master of eluding police, was driving yet another stolen vehicle. He knew that one jurisdiction's officers couldn't follow him into another city's limits without a justifiable reason. Whatever might be wrong with this car—expired plates, no taillight, or whatever the officer suspected—would not be enough to be followed into Kansas City. He had an odd talent for stealing cars and auto parts, which again benefitted him. He would, however, leave a telltale clue in the car that would link him to the crime. His days of auto theft were about to come to a halt, but not before he committed one last, horrific offense that would forever change the course of local history. His all-night-into-early morning crime spree was the last night of peaceful slumber the Harrisons would ever know.

There were stolen "T-tops" in the car that the pair had planned to sell at a "chop shop"—a covert operation that dealt in stolen auto parts in Raytown, Missouri. Instead, because the business was not open yet, they drove around to kill time, or at least they claimed that was all they planned to kill. It was the only reason that they were in the neighborhood.

About 7:00 a.m., they saw fifteen-year-old Ann Marie Harrison waiting for the school bus at the end of her driveway. Taylor told Nunley, who was driving at the time, to stop so Taylor could snatch her purse. Nunley stopped the car, Taylor got out, pretended to need directions, grabbed her, and put her in the front seat between himself and Nunley. He left her purse and other belongings exactly where she had placed them. They remained undisturbed. Nunley would later reveal that Taylor was not interested in a theft. His intentions were far more sinister.

A neighbor would later state that at approximately 7:06 a.m., he heard two screams—one loud and terrifying, the other cut off with the slamming of a car door. He would recall that he heard the vehicle speed off and glimpsed a Chevy through his kitchen window. Once in the car, Taylor blindfolded Ann with his sock and threatened to stab her with a screwdriver if she was not quiet. Nunley drove to his mother's house in Grandview, Missouri, and pulled the car into the garage at the back of the residence. Nunley bound her hands with cable wire and took Ann to the basement. The evidence adduced in Taylor's sentencing hearing reveals a different factual version of the crime than the evidence offered in Nunley's proceedings.

Taylor claimed that Nunley first removed Ann's clothes and had forcible sexual intercourse with her. Taylor said he remained in the garage while this happened, and then he, Taylor, had forcible intercourse with her. They finally untied her and allowed her to dress. Ann tried to persuade them to call her parents for ransom, and Nunley promised he would take her to a telephone to call home. They once again blindfolded her, re-tied her hands, and led her to the trunk of the Monte Carlo. Ann resisted getting into the trunk until Nunley told her it was a necessary step so that no one would see her. Both men helped her into the trunk. Nunley then returned to the house for two knives: a butcher knife, and a smaller steak knife. Nunley argued with Taylor about whether to kill her. Taylor only wanted to rape her and let her go. Conversely, Nunley did not want Ann to testify against him and emphasized he and Taylor were in this together. After all, it was his fault that Ann knew his name; Taylor's the one who called out to him, asking him to retrieve some hair gel so that he could use it as a disgusting aid in the rape process.

Nunley attempted to slash her throat after bringing the knives from the kitchen, but the blade was too dull. So instead, he stabbed her through the throat and told Taylor to "stick her." The medical examiner would later conclude that Nunley had not only driven the knife from one side of Ann's neck to the other but that he twisted the knife, adding insult to her deadly wounds. It just solidified the knowledge that Nunley was a violent, menacing creature with no conscience. It was not the first time he killed, and his time in prison would reveal that it wouldn't be the last time he would try. As Nunley continued to stab at her body, Taylor stabbed Ann "two or three times, probably four." He described how "her eyes rolled up in her head, and she was sort of like trying to catch her, her breath."

Nunley and Taylor argued about who would drive the Monte Carlo, and Nunley ended up driving it. Nunley liked to be in control, and he could usually intimidate his companions into allowing him to operate whatever vehicle they were using. As Nunley left the garage in the stolen Monte Carlo with the victim's body still in the trunk, Taylor followed Nunley in another stolen automobile, a Buick Riviera that they would also end up abandoning.

At around 8:30 a.m., an hour and a half after they kidnapped Ann, Nunley abandoned the automobile on a street, just a little over half of a mile from Taylor's mother's house. Nunley then got into the stolen car that Taylor had been driving, and they returned to the home of Nunley's mother, where Ann had been brutalized just a short time earlier. It was as though nothing significant had happened; it was just business as usual. The two killers then got rid of the murder weapons, the bloodstained sock used as a blindfold, and the binding cable they removed from Ann after she was murdered. Nunley and Taylor had grabbed Ann from the curb where she innocently waited for her school bus and, a mere ninety minutes later, dumped the vehicle containing her ravaged and mutilated body, leaving her to die alone by the side of the road.

✴

Taylor's initial post-conviction hearing was held before Judge Dierker on January 3, 1992.

The following is Taylor's testimony on cross-examination at the post-conviction hearing:

Q. Well, did you think that your chances of not getting death were really good in front of a jury?

A. I knew that I did not want to go in front of a jury.

Q. And why was that, Mr. Taylor?

A. Because I was admitting my guilt.

Q. I'm not talking about the issue of guilt. I'm talking about the issue of punishment. Did you want to go in front of a jury for them to decide whether you would live or die?

A. Not then, but now I do.

Two subsequent hearings would be held in March 1992 before Judge Dierker finally handed down his decision. Judge Dierker ruled on the appropriateness of the plea entered by Taylor and the subsequent sentences imposed by Judge Randall. Judge Dierker upheld Judge Randall's decisions. Taylor's appeal was denied in July 1992, and Taylor was re-sentenced to death. Nunley's attorneys had petitioned the Judge for a post-conviction relief hearing, and it was also rejected.

Two more appeals were filed with the Jackson County Circuit Court; Judge H. Michael Coburn heard the first in 1993. That hearing was held in 1994, and the prosecution presented evidence of Ann's kidnapping, rape, and murder. Prosecutors also presented evidence surrounding Taylor's escape from custody after his arrest for Ann's murder. Judge Coburn denied Taylor's motion to withdraw his guilty plea. Instead, he re-sentenced Taylor to death for the murder conviction, fifteen years for the kidnapping conviction, life for the rape conviction, and fifty years for the armed criminal action conviction. The sentences were all to run consecutively. After unsuccessfully launching this appeal, Taylor's attorneys filed yet another motion, this time to be heard by Judge Edith Messina. Her ruling was the same as Judge Coburn's.

CHAPTER 17

As with everything that seemed to touch this case, another tragedy befell one individual close to it. Judge H. Michael Coburn, who ruled on one of the many appeals filed on behalf of Ann's killers, was not exempt from misfortune. On December 23, 1994, Judge Coburn went to personally inspect a condemned building site that was the basis for a temporary restraining order filed for his review and signature.

The City of Kansas City, Missouri, tried to get the owner to complete the half-finished building or tear it down. City officials, representatives from neighborhood groups who complained about the dangerous site, the owner, and his lawyer all gathered at 8:30 a.m. on the day before Christmas Eve to look at the site. Upon entering the building and walking a short distance, Judge Coburn fell into an open stairwell that had previously been barricaded. Although he had a flashlight, the Judge could not see the hazard in front of him. Because of the removal of the safety barrier, he fell about 12 feet and sustained head injuries that would prove fatal some four days later. Attorneys representing the Coburn family successfully defended a lawsuit against the building owner, proving negligence by the building owner. Tragedy was never far from the Harrison case.

✻

In January 1994, Nunley had a hearing before Judge John O'Malley to withdraw his guilty plea, but by May of that year, Judge O'Malley denied it and sentenced Nunley to death. Following that defeat, Nunley's attorneys filed another motion for post-conviction relief. This time, they would present it to the judge in February and be denied by O'Malley in March.

The state's highest court initially scheduled Nunley to die in September 1996. But three days before the execution, the same court stayed their order pending further review in state and federal courts.

The ruling for Nunley was final on September 17, 1996, which panicked Taylor and his attorneys. The State set his execution for January 3, 1997, and they felt they were running out of time. Fortunately for Taylor, his attorneys filed with the Federal Courts for an appeal, and they granted him a stay of execution pending the High Court's ruling. The United States Supreme Court, however, denied discretionary review. This on-again, off-again pattern would continue for the next 26 years. Between the two murderers, a combined total of eighty actions pertained to the Ann Harrison murder case.

The next step for Taylor's attorney was to file a motion with the Missouri Supreme Court. In the case of the State v Taylor 929 S.W.2d 209 (Mo.1996) the court held that: (1) defendant did not suffer manifest injustice as result of fact he was sentenced by a different judge than one before whom he had pled guilty; (2) defendant was not entitled to withdraw his plea on grounds of inadequate personal admonition; (3) defendant could not withdraw his plea on grounds that he was not advised that his intent to kill victim was (sic) element of first-degree murder; (4) there was sufficient evidence of defendant's deliberation and culpable intent to warrant acceptance of defendant's plea; (5) defendant was not entitled to jury on resentencing following remand; (6) recusal of resentencing and post-conviction judges was not required; (7) defendant failed to establish that prosecutor had acted with racially discriminatory purpose in deciding to seek death penalty; (8) post-conviction judge properly found that mitigation investigation was adequate; and (9) defense counsel's failure to make further mitigation investigation was not ineffective assistance of counsel.

⁑

The first scheduled execution day for Michael Taylor was in February 2006. It brought with it a rollercoaster of emotions for the friends who represented the Harrisons that day. Bob and Janel Harrison had planned to travel to Bonne Terre but decided against it. Their friends who served as their representatives were witnesses for the State of Missouri, and no one from Ann's family was going to attend.

Al DeValkenaere intended to witness the execution of the killer he worked so diligently to identify and put behind bars.

DeValkenaere spent six years as a detective in the Homicide Unit and got over seventy confessions from suspects. He was recruited by Troy Cole when Cole, a former homicide detective, transferred back to Homicide as a sergeant. Trained by Detective Bill Wilson, DeValkenaere worked the Bob Berdella serial killer case with Cole. When Pete Edlund returned to the Homicide Unit at Van Buskirk's request, squads were divided up, and he was assigned to Edlund.

It is frequently the case that command staff from various agencies will excessively pressure their detectives to rapidly solve high-profile crimes, calling multiple times a day for updates, insisting upon overtime, additional staffing, etc. In this instance, no undue pressure was applied. The chief of police trusted Gary Van Buskirk, confident in his leadership and his team's abilities. However, each detective was experiencing their own self-imposed pressure to find Ann's killers. This murder was a case of an utterly unsuspecting victim, someone who was not in the act of committing a crime or who had placed herself in harm's way, knowing that she was undertaking a risk. She was a little girl standing at the edge of her driveway as she kept to herself and waited for the bus to take her to school. She never got the chance to grow up.

As DeValkenaere described it, "Ann was special." He still keeps a basket of mementos from some of his cases, and in it is a Polaroid picture of Ann that he carried in his pocket for years. It was a copy of her sophomore school picture distributed to all the investigators when she first went missing.

What troubled DeValkenaere the most was asking, "What else could I have done today to clear this case? What other stone could have been overturned? Where else could I have looked?"

This introspection was a consistent theme among all the detectives working the case.

According to DeValkenaere, his serving as the lead detective was simply because he wrote the initial report and the case was assigned to him. He had been in the unit for two years. Pete called and gave his usual "Saddle up" notice to his squad. DeValkenaere lived close to where the car with Ann's body was discovered, enabling him to respond within minutes.

He worked every stolen auto, gleaning information from the tactical squads who gathered specific information for the homicide unit. Nunley and Taylor's method of stealing T-Tops, removing dome lights and ashtrays, was of particular interest. The case brought forth oddities and sometimes a little craziness. Psychics, known sex offenders, bloodhounds, cadaver dogs, whatever the lead, the Murder Squad took every opportunity to run it down.

DeValkenaere attended every court session that he could, but this was limited. He was also testifying; therefore, could not be in the courtroom for much of the case, but the case never left him.

CHAPTER 18

Al DeValkenaere had waited seventeen years for this day to come finally. But unfortunately, it was not closure he expected as much as it was a closing of a book whose long-overdue final chapter could now be written.

Two of Bob and Janel Harrison's friends assumed the roles of cross bearers to take a load off Ann's parents, if only for this moment in time. But, like Simon of Cyrene, it was only a brief respite that was provided, as the burden of this cross was to fall back on the Harrisons' shoulders repeatedly before the execution process for Ann's killers would be concluded. What the Harrisons would endure with the start/stop process of executions being scheduled, then stayed, and scheduled again was excruciating, cruel, and unnecessary. The process would repeatedly victimize the already suffering parents for another nine years.

Witnesses had to arrive on Tuesday, January 31 at 10:30 p.m. for the 12:01 a.m. execution on February 1, 2006. Each one received a confirmation letter from the State of Missouri Department of Corrections that provided instructions regarding the execution.

"Dear XXXXXXX:

The purpose of this letter is to confirm your selection to serve as a state witness at the execution of the above referenced inmate at the Eastern Reception Diagnostic & Correctional

Center in Bonne Terre, MO at 12:01 a.m. on Wednesday,
February 6, 2006.

You are to report to the administration building at the
Eastern Reception Diagnostic & Correctional Center on
the evening of Tuesday, January 31st at 10:30 p.m. Upon
your arrival at the administration building, you will be
required to present current identification with picture prior
to admittance to comply with State Statute which requires
witnesses to be citizens who are at least 21 years of age.
Please leave purses, briefcases, cellular phones, cameras,
and any electronic or recording device, etc. in your vehicle
if possible.

Prior to the escort to the witness area, you will be briefed
regarding your duties and responsibilities as a state's
witness.

It is recommended that you call the institution to confirm the
execution date and time before you travel to Bonne Terre,
MO by calling 573-XXX-XXXX."

The three witnesses for the State of Missouri stayed in
St. Louis and drove to Bonne Terre together. The prison
had instructed them to arrive at 6:30 p.m. at the prison's
front gate. Upon arrival, officers at the gate approached the
car and requested identification. There seemed to be some
confusion about allowing the witnesses to enter at that time,
and guards advised them to come back at 8:30 p.m. There
was nowhere to go but a Hardee's fast-food restaurant near
the Interstate. The group left and headed to the restaurant,
but the food was the last thing on anyone's mind. Soft drinks
and a soft-spoken conversation ensued until enough time
had passed to head back to the prison. It was hard to make
small talk with death looming over their heads.

When they returned to the prison, the identification
process was repeated twice; the first stop at the gate and

a second check about 50 feet into the parking area, where guards pointed out the designated parking space. The officer indicated that the prisoner's family, the media, and protesters were located on the other side of the building. This slow and meticulous process was intended to mitigate all potential risks of interaction between witnesses, victim and prisoner families, and the protestors. Double-checking and verifying the identities of all the players was the State's equivalent to Bob Vila's "measure twice, cut once" process to eliminate any mistakes. The entire prison was on lockdown for two days before the execution and would remain so for the balance of the week.

A group of representatives from the prison met the three witnesses and escorted them into the facility. Guards said little, and it was primarily to give instructions to sign in, provide identification, and lock up belongings. Then, one at a time, the guards searched them, instructed them to walk through a metal detector, and escorted them down a locked hallway. About halfway down the hall, there was a bulletproof glass window with a dark window film, making it difficult to see the source of the voice you heard on the microphone.

The shadowy figure of a guard was moving behind the glass in a dimly lit control room. He instructed each witness to step up, place the ID in the drawer, and wait. It was high on the wall, and there was a slide-out drawer to put identification in for the guard to inspect. He would look at the person's information, then look up at the individual waiting on the other side and then send the ID back out and give the exact instructions to the next in line. Because he was hard to see, one had to wonder if his expression questioned the information on the identification provided or if he held any expression at all. It was, after all, the State's intake center for new prisoners, and the witnesses described it as feeling like convicts as they were marched down the hall and out into an open-air connector to the next building, replete with chain link and razor wire. As the witnesses walked the "gray mile" to the Missouri death chamber, no words were spoken.

Once all the parties had entered the second building, the door slammed shut with a thundering sound reminiscent of a 1950s Hollywood film noir. The escort continued past a large room with tables and vending machines lining the walls with goods accessible to prisoners if they possessed enough coins to insert into the machines. It was the visiting area for prisoners. A locker room adjacent to that corridor provided access to the witness waiting area. Every time they entered a new location, a door slammed shut behind the group as they waited for a guard to unlock the next door and lead them again. The clanging sound of the doors closing against any chance of retreat while giving off a sense of finality did not make one feel secure, only uncertain.

The cinderblock witness room was some institutional shade of colorless. There was a restroom inside the space, which was of some comfort, as they provided witnesses with an endless stream of water and some jailhouse coffee that was dark and tasteless, not unlike the décor in the room. The coffee lent itself to giving new meaning to the term "correction fluid."

The Department of Corrections provided each witness a 20-page packet of information, including: a photograph and history of the inmate sentenced for execution, circumstances of the offense, legal chronology, history of the death penalty in Missouri, lethal injection statute, a current list of capital punishment inmates since 1979, a current list of capital punishment inmates, and Missouri inmates executed since 1989.

Prison officials had cautioned the guards to speak to witnesses only when spoken to and to give short, if not one word, answers to the witnesses. In addition, the guards could discuss nothing related to the inmate, the execution, or voice personal opinions. Among the witnesses were reporters who served as State witnesses and to document the execution that was about to occur.

At first, there were a few brief conversations among the group, but the level of awkwardness grew into an overwhelming sense of discomfort as the hours passed. Occasionally someone would comment, but then the silence started up again. Only the rattling of papers, the turn of a magazine page, or the clearing of a throat would break the stillness. Only the hands of the institutional wall clock seemed to make any natural movement.

The room's design and the connecting ductwork allowed occupants to overhear muddled conversation in the adjacent room and vice versa. The prisoner's family was waiting in that other room. Nothing could be distinguished clearly, only a word or two now and then. A reporter attempted to make small talk with the other witnesses, speculating on what Taylor was doing, how the impending execution was affecting him, how he spent his time on his last day. The discussion revolved around Taylor, with sympathies being voiced about him.

The author finally spoke up and asked of no one in particular, "Isn't anyone thinking about Ann Harrison and how she spent her last hours on this earth? Isn't that really the reason we are all here?". The room became quiet. Nothing else was said until one reporter finally offered, "This is true. I wonder what the Harrisons must be going through?" As the witnesses continued to wait, if there was any speculation about Ann's family, it was done in silence.

Representatives of the prison entered periodically, huddling near the door to speak before addressing the group, who continued to sit quietly, watching the clock. It was a hushed conversation, not low enough to be a whisper but not at a level to be clearly understood. Then, the most official looking of the group gave an update. He addressed the group four different times, and each time, hearts would pound as each witness readied for the execution. Get ready to go in ten minutes. No, wait. It's off again. It's back on again. Efforts were made to move the execution forward, primarily because a death warrant was for just one day. If the prisoner's execution were not carried out during those 24 hours, the State would have to re-petition the court for another death warrant. Scheduling the execution for 12:01 a.m. gives the State as much time as possible to deal with last-minute legal appeals and temporary stays.

In 2006, his eleventh-hour appeal regarding cruel and unusual punishment by lethal injection was approved to be heard by the 8th U.S. Circuit Court of Appeals, and it granted Taylor a stay. Therefore, on February 1, 2006, Taylor's first execution was postponed. The 8th U.S. Circuit Court of Appeals had granted his stay so the full court could conduct a re-hearing. The United States Supreme Court refused to overturn the stay. Only Chief Justices John Roberts, Antonin Scalia, and Clarence Thomas voted to lift the stay and proceed with the execution.

※

Roderick Nunley would start fights at the prison and get sent to "the hole"—a slang term for getting removed from the general population—as punishment. He was ill-tempered, confrontational, and combative, all of which presented problems for the prison. The U.S. Supreme Court declined to intervene in Nunley's case in 2005, an action which proved to agitate the already belligerent Nunley further.

In 2006, Nunley mauled a manager at the Potosi Correctional Center, where he was being held.

On Monday, January 9, 2006, Nunley caused the entire Potosi Correctional Center to be placed on lockdown. He had been permitted to go to an administrative office to get permission to use the library to seek information regarding his appeal. He had heard that the Missouri Supreme Court had set a date of February 1, 2006, as his new execution date, and therefore he wanted to go to the library. He then attacked one of the prison's functional unit managers with a homemade knife that he had fashioned and stabbed the staff member so horrifically that the victim had to be transported by medical helicopter to a trauma center in St. Louis. The man was working on Nunley's request when the inmate ambushed him. Officials said Nunley stabbed the man in the head, collarbone, and back with a 4- or 5-inch metal shard fashioned into a crude weapon. Although the manager survived his injuries, he suffered long-term effects from the unprovoked attack. Two other staff members suffered minor injuries as they attempted to intervene. Nunley's brilliant idea was to attack a staff member and cause an investigation and thereby delay his execution. Instead, he managed to get himself removed from the general population and placed in administrative segregation until the incident could be investigated. Nunley was just an evil character all around. This was the same individual who not only stabbed Ann in the neck with a serrated knife, but also twisted the knife while stabbing.

Warden Don Roper was quoted in the local news, stating, "Our people do an outstanding job. We do this job in a highly volatile situation. These inmates are dangerous people." Dangerous, indeed. Nunley was a cold-blooded, narcissistic psychopath who placed no value on any human life but his own.

CHAPTER 19

The first time the Missouri Supreme Court scheduled Roderick Nunley's execution was for October 20, 2010.

The process was the same drill that witnesses attending on the Harrisons' behalf went through in 2006 when Michael Taylor's original execution date was set. Witnesses for the State and the Harrison family booked hotel rooms in St. Louis to ensure they wouldn't stay at the same hotel as Nunley's family. Unfortunately, there was no easy way to get from St. Louis to Bonne Terre. The journey consisted of primarily rural roads on the 59-mile stretch between the two cities on the state's eastern side. It was a beautiful autumn day and, had they been there for any other purpose, it might have been an enjoyable drive.

Like the previous trip to Bonne Terre, witnesses were escorted through the chain-link gates by prison security and directed to the designated parking in the building's front. Nothing much had changed. Show picture identification at the front desk and sign the logbook. Lock up personal items in the lockers, take off shoes and go through the stationary metal detector and hand-wanding processes. Again, little was spoken by the same uniformed guards that walked the witnesses through the 2006 process, only this time, this was for the scheduled execution of the other participant in Ann's murder—Roderick Nunley.

If not for Nunley's panic and insistence that she needed to be silenced so as not to identify them, Ann might have been allowed to live. In 1990, the average time of incarceration in Missouri for forcible rape with a weapon or physical injury was 18.4 years, serving 93% of the sentence. That equated to a little over 17 years for the brutality that Ann endured and small consolation, but she still would have been alive. Even adding in her kidnapping for another 11.9 years, of which 75% would have to be served (8.9 years), they'd have both been free before the time the State carried out their actual executions. Of course, this is assuming Nunley did not carry out the violent attack against a prison administrator. For that, Nunley may have remained in prison; he would, however, have avoided the needle. Taylor would have served his time, and Ann would have survived.

Waiting for Nunley's scheduled execution was more of the same; the same terrible coffee in the same cinderblock room, with guards who weren't allowed to do more than listen to the conversations between the State witnesses and the witnesses from the media. The only change was the addition of some packaged cookies that the prison supplied. Perhaps the issue of vending machines had not wholly been lost on prison administration.

Nunley's request for a temporary stay came more quickly than Taylor's had in 2006. The State was scrambling to block it, and there was speculation that it would be successful by the following evening. "Come back tomorrow." Was not that what the guard told Dorothy in *The Wizard of Oz?* So now it felt as though it was just a matter of time before the witnesses would be directed to bring back a witch's broomstick. It was a gut-wrenching, heart-aching process. Hadn't Ann's family and those attending on behalf of the Harrisons waited long enough?

This time, the witnesses were more hopeful and spent the day in St. Genevieve, Missouri, a town steeped in history, with scenery which offered a brief respite from the previous day's frustrations. Perhaps October 21st would be the day of closure on this execution.

Upon returning to St. Louis a little after 4:30 p.m., the plan was to meet up with Al DeValkenaere, grab some dinner, and head back to Bonne Terre. They were to return at 8:30 p.m. to start the process again, but that was not to be.

At 4:45 p.m., the prison called, and witnesses were to get there immediately as it looked like Nunley's execution was occurring at 6:00 p.m. Bonne Terre was an hour away, and it was rush hour in St. Louis. There did not seem to be any way that they could make it in time. So the witnesses were about to embark on what they would remember as the ride of a lifetime.

Divine Providence allowed the three witnesses to arrive at their destination scarcely before the 6:00 p.m. time frame. The guards at the gates expected them and skirted them through as quickly as possible. Despite the whispered prayers and skilled maneuvering through the traffic lanes filled with endless vehicles, there was to be no resolution today.

Although the Missouri Supreme Court denied the stay of execution application filed by his attorneys, the United States District Court for the Western District of Missouri granted the stay. This time, Nunley's team would argue that he was entitled to have a jury decide his sentence even though he and his attorneys opted not to go before a jury due to the heinous nature of his crime.

The wheels of justice had almost ground to a halt as Nunley was granted one more break that would grind through the courts for another four years. It became increasingly harder to hold fast to the belief that good triumphs over evil when evil seemed to keep scoring all the goals.

Adrenaline was pumping, flooding the witnesses with a panoply of emotions. This time, the guards not only escorted them to their vehicle, one older officer stopped and waited for the appropriate moment to speak. Then, sidling up to the Harrisons' representatives and speaking in a low voice, he said, "Don't worry. We'll get him sooner or later."

The wheels of justice had ground to a stop; once for Taylor and now for Nunley. However, the guard's prediction was a reassurance that these same wheels would somehow turn once more and bring a conclusion to what now felt like a recurring nightmare. Those simple words whispered in the briskness of an early fall morning offered more comfort than he could ever have imagined.

CHAPTER 20

It would be another four years before anything tangible surfaced from the Department of Corrections. Then, finally, the Harrison family was notified that an execution date for Michael Taylor was scheduled for the end of February 2014.

Ann's youngest sister, Lisa, crafted a tribute to her sister and posted it on Facebook. It reads:

"February 25, 2014

I'm a very private person and will usually opt to not doing any of this so public, but I feel the time is right, and I hope that a different approach to coping with this execution will mean it will actually happen.

If I could vocalize everything I am about to say, I would thank each and every one of you in person. I just know I would never get the words out without busting out in an uncontrollable, messy cry. Although I know many of you would make time for it, I will say for comedic purposes, that ain't nobody got time for that.

A wholehearted thank you goes out to many lately. Thank you for keeping my family in your thoughts. Thank you for those of you who have kept Ann's memory alive. Thank you for posting pictures and for planning events to celebrate her life. I hope to gain the courage to join you and hear stories about her.

I don't have very many memories of Ann. Even the memories I have, I am unsure if I generated them so I could at least feel like I knew her. Through stories told by my family, I know she was a very caring and patient person, traits most exercised when dealing with a very terrible, toddler Lisa. I know she loved playing her flute, her memory that lived on as Debra played her flute throughout school. Ann loved softball, where an annual softball tournament would bring together family and friends and people who knew her to remember her. These are just a few examples of how Ann continued to be a part of my life, not for how she died, but for who she was.

For 25 years, thank you to her friends and teachers for staying in touch with my family, sending cards and pink roses to let us know they are thinking of her. To the teachers we had, that even with the occasional slip of calling me Ann in class, I could never be mad because it was always a compliment. To her closest friends, David and Juliet, that, without hesitation, kept us so close to them that I have always considered them honorary siblings, doing things that older siblings should do, like teaching us how to not listen to crappy music and how to play the most fantastic game of Lava using living room furniture while the parents were out.

Most of all, to my parents, thank you for being so strong, to face hell and refusing to let it shut you down. Thank you for providing Debra and I with the most normal childhood you could. We had to learn first-hand how evil people can be and had our innocence taken from us at a very young age. You still taught us how beautiful the world is, and there is still joy to be had and good memories to be made. Thank you for showing us that when difficult times are faced, we still stand on our two feet and it's okay to cry. Thank you for fighting so hard and being strong to bring justice for Ann.

Thank you for telling me the times I remind you of her, our similar laughs and similar sense of humor.

Tonight, I am full of emotions. A heavy heart knowing what Ann's last moment (sic) were like. Angry that it has taken so long for this to happen. Anxious not knowing if the execution will happen, and that if it does, we will go through this again with Nunley. Ready for the day that I will never have to see their faces or hear their names. And someday, hopefully, peace."

❈

It was February 26, 2014, and the correctional center was on lockdown. It had been locked down the day before and would remain so the next day if the evening's scheduled execution occurred. This would be the third time it planned an execution for one or the other of Ann's killers. No one knew if it would proceed this time. In another twist of irony, it was scheduled two days after what would have been Ann's 40th birthday. Yet another milestone on this road that she would never travel.

At approximately 6:40 p.m., Missouri Governor Jay Nixon denied clemency for Michael Taylor, and the execution was to proceed as scheduled at 12:01 a.m. the following morning. During his tenure as governor of Missouri, Jay Nixon had denied clemency for many other death row inmates, and Taylor would prove to be no exception.

His office issued the Governor's statement, which read:

"I have received from my counsel a final briefing on the petition for clemency from Michael Taylor, which has been reviewed in detail. After careful deliberation, I have denied this petition. As Governor, this is a power and a process I do not take lightly. Each instance involves a very specific set of facts, which must be considered on its own."

"Fifteen-year-old Ann Harrison was waiting for the school bus at the end of her driveway when she was abducted, raped, and then stabbed to death by Michael Taylor and Roderick Nunley. Years later, the brutality of this crime and the loss of this innocent child remain seared in the memory of the Harrison family and many Kansas City residents. Taylor pleaded guilty to these wanton, heinous crimes and was subsequently convicted of murder and sentenced to death. My decision today upholds this appropriate sentence."

"I ask that Missourians remember Ann Harrison at this time and keep her parents, Bob and Janel Harrison, and the Harrison family in your thoughts and prayers."

⁕

This trip to Bonne Terre differed from the previous ones. The Harrisons traveled there for the execution, and Bob's brother, David, and sister Ann and her husband, planned to meet them there. Their friends who had made this trip multiple times over the years would also travel the 300 miles to the death house again to see if the appeals would be exhausted, and justice would finally be meted out for the instigator of the horrific events that led to Ann's murder. They arrived at the hotel in Farmington in the early afternoon. Experience had taught them not to stay in St. Louis, as proximity to the prison was vital, given the erratic on/off pattern of appeals.

Al DeValkenaere drove down by himself and went directly to the prison. He planned to drive back to Kansas City immediately after the execution. He wanted time and distance to process what he had waited more than a quarter of a century for.

The Harrisons arrived late in the afternoon and met Bob's sister and her husband at the hotel. David Harrison flew into St. Louis from a meeting with an out-of-state client. He then drove from St. Louis; the last to arrive at the prison. He would depart after the execution and make the drive back to St. Louis to catch an early morning flight.

They decided that the group, minus Al and David, would meet at the local Applebee's for dinner before leaving for Bonne Terre. Bob's sister, Ann, would stay behind at the hotel with Janel after dinner, as Janel elected not to attend the execution itself.

The dinner conversation was polite yet somewhat stilted. Discussions revolved around the drive down, the excellent weather, and the food quality. Oddly, all the meals were finished despite no one having the appetite for watching a man die. Dining was simply something that needed to be done so everyone went through the motions.

The Eastern Reception, Diagnostic and Correctional Center in Bonne Terre houses over 2,500 prisoners and is the facility where new prisoners are inducted into the correctional system after sentencing. In addition, it operates a cooked and chilled food facility that prepares and transports all inmate meals to the Missouri Eastern, Potosi, and Farmington Correctional Centers, as well as the St. Louis Community Release Center. It also houses the lethal injection execution chamber moved from the Potosi Correctional Center in 2005.

While awaiting the scheduling of their execution dates, the inmates on death row are a part of the general population at Potosi, where they work in the prison laundry and have access to the law library, the gymnasium, and other facilities that any other prisoner could use. The death row prisoners remain housed at Potosi until being moved to Bonne Terre shortly before their scheduled execution.

Taylor did not use his right to request a specific last meal. When nothing special is asked for, the prison serves the prisoner whatever meal is available. In this case, it was potato soup and a sandwich. Taylor was convinced that he would eat breakfast back at the Potosi Correctional Center at the prison some 18 miles west, and all would be right again in his world.

He bragged to the guards at the prison that he would receive yet another stay of execution and he would be back at the party by morning. The braggadocio did not know that his career as a criminal was circling the drain in these last hours. In fact, so was Taylor.

⁂

Back at the hotel, witnesses planned to travel to the prison in one car, and Dave Bernard drove the group. Although he used his Garmin for directions, it was a route that he was already familiar with, having taken it multiple times before. Unfortunately, the prior trips were unproductive, but perhaps the road would lead to a resolution, at least for one of Ann's killers.

It had been a reasonably mild day for late February in Missouri. The temperature had risen to 36°F in the afternoon, and it was still comfortable as the group traveled to the prison. A female voice from the directional device spoke which direction to travel and where to turn when required. Sixteen miles and twenty-two minutes were the length and time expected to arrive at the destination. Rather than directing to Highway K and straight to the prison, the voice gave instructions to exit at Orchard Road and follow it to the right.

About that time, the wind picked up, and it began snowing large, heavy flakes, and visibility was limited. It was as though there was something in the air that changed as the passengers got closer to the prison, with its bright lights casting an eerie yellow glow in the distance. What had been a still, dry night was now covered in snow, a wailing wind that sent a chill through the soul. That route took the car to a street called Stormy Lane, a moniker befitting the circumstance, where it dead-headed directly toward the

Gospel Light Free Will Baptist Church. The church's sign was illuminated and seemed to provide a guiding light to get the travelers back on the road in the correct direction. Again, the experience seemed surreal, as though Hell was freezing over. Perhaps this time, unlike all the times before, the execution would proceed as planned.

Before his execution, Taylor provided a statement to Reuters. "I hurt for her family… No words can express the pain and anguish that they have lived with through the years. I can only wish them peace and pray there will come a day when they can forgive me." Taylor did not offer any other final words at his execution but had earlier claimed that he had written an apology letter to the Harrisons. However, no such letter was ever provided.

CHAPTER 21

At the age of 47, Michael Taylor was executed on February 26, 2014 at 12:10 a.m. for Ann's murder. There were many last-minute petitions to the U.S. Supreme Court to gain yet another stay, but there was no more time to buy. He received his lethal injection despite the best efforts of his attorneys, who fought to convince the courts that this method of execution was a slow and excruciating death. A slow and excruciating death better described what Ann had endured as she fought to stay alive as her kidnappers stabbed her repeatedly and left her to die some two hours later. She remained conscious for at least fifteen minutes, according to the medical examiner. Fifteen horrifying minutes to know she was dying. Fifteen agonizing minutes to suffer the pain from those massive injuries inflicted upon her by Michael Taylor. Fifteen minutes to endure the pain from the rape that tore her both internally and externally. Fifteen minutes to cry silently for her parents—an inaudible lament as her injuries rendered her voiceless.

Taylor did not suffer an unspeakable and inhumane death in a dirty car trunk. He did not lie there blindfolded, helpless, and terrified while his murderers joked about how to carry out the killing. That horror was reserved only for his victim. No, he was to have a team of medical professionals clad in clinical garb administer his drugs in a clean, sterile room. They would lay him out on a medical gurney covered, neck to toe, with clean, snow-white sheets. In a macabre piece of irony, his arm was wiped with an alcohol swab before his I.V. was started to prevent the possibility of injection site infection. Taylor was not wearing his clothes inside out, nor was he blindfolded with a dirty sock and forced, terrified and bleeding from insufferable brutality, to crawl on his hands and knees as he faced certain death. No, that was what he forced his victim to endure. Ann suffered.

There was no vast amount of medical equipment surrounding him; only one singular cord dangled from under the sheet into a connection on the wall behind him visible to the witnesses. Taylor looked to his left and mouthed something to his family, seated behind a glass window in a darkened room, and then looked at the ceiling. He turned his head once more to the left, then turned it back, straight ahead, and closed his eyes. He took two long breaths, and then the rise and fall of his chest stopped; all visible signs of his breathing had disappeared. In less than nine minutes from the moment the process began, his heart ceased to beat. It was 12:10 a.m.

Taylor was the second execution in 2014. He was number 72 since Missouri reinstated executions decades earlier. Both the families of the victim and the killer gave statements to the media.

Taylor's family elected to provide a quote to the press.

"The family of Michael Anthony Taylor would like to express their gratitude to all of those who supported Michael over the years. It may be a small victory for the State of Missouri, but Michael has won in the end. He has struggled for years with the guilt of not stopping a horrendous crime, and has dedicated much of his time in prison to the memory of Ann Harrison through his work with hospice, tutoring, and mentoring inside and outside the prison wall. Those heartfelt accomplishments will accompany him into the gates of Heaven where he will be joined by his family and beloved angel."

Prison employees gave a far different version of Taylor's days behind bars and stated that he was so confident that he would not be executed, Taylor told guards he would "be back at Potosi by morning." His arrogance was not diminished by time or incarceration. Taylor was neither the model prisoner nor mentor that his family claimed. He participated in the same covert crimes that other prisoners committed. He sincerely believed that he would avoid the death penalty and bragged about it.

Janel Harrison also provided a statement to the press. "Regarding Taylor spending the rest of his life in prison... when you commit the ultimate crime, which is murder, then there should be an ultimate penalty. If Ann had been allowed to live, Taylor would have received a life sentence."

Under State of Missouri sentencing guidelines, the aggravating circumstances of Ann's murder, coupled with the prior criminal histories of the killers, would have resulted in life without parole. Additionally, forcible rape, kidnapping, and first-degree assault were classified as dangerous felonies. These were two individuals who should have spent their lives in prison for their crimes, but had they shown Ann mercy enough to allow her to live, they would also have been afforded the privilege of life.

Taylor believed he would escape the death sentence being carried out because, in 2006, his eleventh-hour appeal to the 8th U.S. Circuit Court of Appeals regarding cruel and unusual punishment by lethal injection gained him a stay of execution. However, two years later, the U.S. Supreme Court would uphold the constitutionality of Missouri's execution process, so his chance of any new appeal being upheld was not realistic.

After the execution, Missouri Governor Jay Nixon released this statement:

"Our thoughts and prayers tonight are with Bob and Janel Harrison, and the other members of Ann Harrison's family,

as they remember the 15-year-old child they lost to an act of senseless violence."

⁑

When Michael Taylor was executed after being on death row for a quarter of a century, he was incarcerated ten years longer than his rape/murder victim lived on earth. He knew his death was imminent: he was provided with a last meal, he could say goodbye to his family, he was treated with dignity, and he went gently into that long goodnight. He did not suffer. Ann suffered.

Taylor stabbed Ann Harrison repeatedly with the steak knife. She was alive during each of those ten stabbings. Tennessee Williams wrote that: "Deliberate cruelty is unforgivable." Ann's killers showed no remorse as they watched the life slowly fade from her suffering body. They inflicted their damage gradually, methodically, and deliberately. In a sickening twist of fate, Nunley admitted twisting his knife after plunging it into Ann's neck.

As previously stated from the autopsy reports, she lived approximately two more hours, having endured six stab wounds to her chest, side, and back. These wounds punctured her heart, lungs, and other organs. She also had four stab wounds to her neck and was so violently raped that her vagina was severely lacerated. Taylor stated he watched her struggle to breathe as she lay bleeding in the trunk of the stolen car. Any reasonable and prudent individual would consider the pain and terror she endured as nothing less than horrific.

Taylor's was not the case of a wrongly accused prisoner on death row based on circumstantial evidence. From the time of his arrest, Taylor pleaded guilty to his crimes, and there was also witness testimony. But most significant was the fact that critical DNA evidence obtained from the victim and her attackers proved beyond any doubt that both

Taylor and his accomplice, Roderick Nunley, had abducted, violently raped, and brutally murdered 15-year-old Ann Marie Harrison.

The victim's head and pubic hairs were at the scene of the rape, which occurred in the basement of the house belonging to Nunley's mother. In addition, blood-typing and DNA testing of semen found in the victim's genitals and on her clothing confirmed that it came from Taylor. There was also physical evidence that proved that Nunley also took part in the attacks. However, he admitted that the drugs he'd been using on the previous night's escapade rendered him incapable of completing the sexual assault that Taylor goaded him on to do.

Public perception is that these individuals are locked away in small, single cells as they repent for their misdeeds. This image was clearly not the case, as these killers had access to socialize with other prisoners, participate in activities, and even obtain contraband. There was a story in the local press about how Taylor found religion in prison and visited hospice patients in the prison hospital. It was another "young man gone wrong" story of repentance, but Taylor came from a good, loving family.

Witnesses learned from the prison staff that both Nunley and Taylor had access to sex and drugs, so nothing changed in their lives from a lifestyle standpoint except that they were now restricted to a smaller footprint than the unsuspecting streets of Kansas City. Their conduct remained the same; only their addresses had changed. However, the lives of the families that live on those unsuspecting streets have been changed forever as the sense of being safe in your own front yard was shattered.

There is no "green mile" where repentant prisoners linger and bond with their jailers. No prayerful activist nun reaches to touch the glass as the condemned man is raised on the gurney in a crucifixion-like manner to utter a poignant apology. Such are the romanticized adaptations of

Hollywood screenwriters. No, what there was instead was a surreal sense of peace and silence.

The drugs administered to the individual are the same used for physician-assisted suicide, legal in the Netherlands and Washington State. It is reasonable to believe that no one seeking to die from unbearable pain through this method of suicide would elect a technique that is "cruel and unusual." It is problematic as a method of execution primarily because laws prevent physicians from administering the drugs required for the process.

In Taylor's case, guards escorted witnesses into a dark room where they sat on folding chairs facing a window with drawn curtains. There were two sets of curtains, one on each side of the glass. Not knowing what to expect, the group sat there for fifteen minutes, and at precisely one minute after midnight, prison staff opened the curtains. Seated facing the prisoner's right side, the observers were approximately ten feet away from him. There was another set of windows on the opposite side of the room where he lay, face-up and covered with a crisp white sheet just below his neck. He turned his head to the left and appeared to be saying something to the witnesses from his family seated on the other side of that glass section. However, no one outside the glass could hear him because of the room's design. He turned his head back toward the ceiling, looked to the left once more, and then back at the ceiling as he closed his eyes. He never moved again.

At roughly seven minutes after midnight, the curtains closed. Witnesses sat and waited silently in the dimly lighted room, listening as the prison director spoke softly on his headset at the back of the room. He softly repeated to his contact, "Time of death, twelve minutes after midnight."

The curtains were re-opened briefly and then were closed once again. The door to the observation room was opened as a prison guard simply said, "Watch your step," escorting his charges back to the holding room so that they could sign the logbook and the death warrant. There was nothing more to say. It was like the words to an old Peggy Lee song, "Is That All There Is?" Is that all there is to an execution?

No one wanted to see anyone suffer, and Taylor got much better than he deserved. He died as dignified a death as one could hope for, in clean surroundings, with his loved ones there to bid a final adieu. Conversely, Ann Harrison suffered. She was terrified, tortured, raped, and stabbed. She begged for her family and cried for her mother. Finally, she was tossed into the trunk of a stolen car and discarded like an old rag doll. Society cannot lose sight of Ann's suffering nor lose sight of the torture that her parents have endured over the last 25 years, as appeal after appeal and execution date after execution date has come and gone.

Ann Harrison did not receive justice with the death of Michael Taylor, nor would justice be served when Roderick Nunley was executed. These actions were reckoning—settling debts owed to society, the family, and Ann. Mr. Taylor received payback as well. And payback is Hell.

CHAPTER 22

In 2014, the Missouri Department of Corrections, the parents of Ann Harrison, and two witnesses scheduled to attend Roderick Nunley's execution were subpoenaed to Missouri Circuit Court in Jefferson City when the American Civil Liberties Union of Missouri filed an action under the Missouri Sunshine Law. The intent was to overturn the confidentiality of how executions are conducted, relative to the privacy of witnesses at the execution who "vouch for its narrative that those killed by the State do not suffer."

The ACLU called into question how the State of Missouri selected its witnesses. It was an opportunity for the ACLU to grandstand about the death penalty, as the Harrisons had every right to attend, two of the witnesses were there on behalf of the Harrisons, and of course, Department of Corrections witnesses went without saying.

The media representatives who attended as witnesses were not named in this action, nor were the offender's family witnesses. Who better to share any irregularities in the execution process of offenders than members of the offender's family? It quickly appeared that this was most likely a ploy, with the actual intent to get personal information that the ACLU could share publicly to pressure witnesses not to attend.

A self-proclaimed community activist from the ACLU was one plaintiff. He stated under oath that he wasn't sure what he wanted to do with the information but stated he might seek out potential witnesses to "discuss" the realities of the death penalty with those individuals. His evasiveness regarding what he was planning to do with the information was clear that he was walking the vainest razor's edge not to be accused of potential witness intimidation—witnesses for Ann. He could not clearly articulate the ACLU's intention for accessing this information, why the media representatives' personal data was not in question, how the information would be used, or the extent of its use.

When prompted, he said having the home and work addresses were necessary to contact witnesses. He admitted that showing up at a witness's home or place of employment was not out of the question. The dangers posed to witnesses were limitless. It would only take one phone call from the offender to wreak havoc, threats, and actions not out of the realm of possibility. What boggled the mind was that this was an attempt also to gather personal information regarding prison employees who might witness the executions. Making this information readily available put guards in an untenable position, as any inmate who held a grudge against a guard who happened to be a witness would now potentially be able to cause harm to them outside the prison walls.

The following are part of the correspondence sent regarding the action taken relative to the disclosure of personal information by the potential witnesses.

Document 1:

May 2, 2014

Custodian of Records

Missouri Department of Corrections

2779 Plaza Drive

Jefferson City, Missouri 65102

By Mail and Facsimile: (573) 751-4099

Subject: Sunshine Law Request

This letter is a request for copies of public records under the Missouri Sunshine Law. Pursuant to the provisions of Chapter 610 of the Missouri Revised Statutes, we request that you provide copies of any and all records in the possession of the Department of Corrections (DOC), regardless of who produced them, regarding witnesses to executions:

1. All records indicating or identifying invitees of the Director (sic) of the Department of Corrections to witness scheduled executions in the past 12 months;

2. All records indicating responses of invitees of the director of the department of corrections (sic) to witness scheduled executions in the past 12 months;

3. All records indicating requests by the public or the media to witness executions in the past 12 months;

4. All records indicating consideration of the requests by the public or the media to witness executions in the past 12 months:

5. All records indicating responses to requests by the public or the media to witness executions in the past 12 months; and

6. All records indicating actual witnesses to executions in the past 12 months.

If any or part of this request is denied, please send a letter listing the specific exemptions upon which you rely for each denial and provide the contact information for the official to whom we may appeal. Mo. Rev. Stat. §610.023.4. This request must "be acted upon as soon as possible, but in no event later than the end of the third business day following the date the request is received." Mo. Rev. Stat. §610.023.3.

Because this records request is being submitted in the public interest and "is likely to contribute significantly to public understanding of the operation or activities" of your department, we ask that you waive any fees or charge a substantially reduced fee pursuant to Mo. Rev. Stat. §610.026.1 (1). However, should you decline to waive or reduce fees, proceed without approval if the cost does not exceed $50.00 and send an invoice with the records. If the cost will exceed $50.00, please inform us of the cost in advance.

All correspondence regarding this request should be send to (executive director).

Thank you for your attention to this matter. If you have any questions, do not hesitate to contact us.

Document 2:

IN THE CIRCUIT COURT OF COLE COUNTY STATE OF MISSOURI

AMERICAN CIVIL LIBERTIES UNION OF MISSOURI, et al

Plaintiffs,

Case No. 14AC-CC00458

MISSOURI DEPARTMENT OF

CORRECTIONS

Defendant.

AFFIDAVIT OF Marla Bernard

I, Marla Bernard (sic) *being first duly sworn, states as follows:*

1.   *am over 18 years of age and competent to make this statement.*

2.   *it is my understanding that Plaintiffs in this case are requesting the release of Department of Corrections' documents containing my personal information, including my home address, date of birth, social security number, place of employment, and criminal history. This information was provided by me so that I could witness the execution of Michael Taylor who murdered my friends' daughter.* (sic) *Ann Harrison.*

3.   *When I completed the application to witness the execution, I never expected that the information I provided could be made public by the ACLU or anyone else.*

4.   *For this reason, I wish to assert any right to privacy that might exist with respect to the un-redacted release of this information.*

5.   *Specifically, I have the following concerns relating to the release of this information:*

I am a retired law enforcement officer who served with the Kansas City, Missouri Police Department for 10 years. During the time that I served as a member of law enforcement, I have made arrests that resulted in the incarceration of many violent criminals. I have always been protective of my personal information in order to protect myself and my family from vengeful persons. I especially have concerns for my daughter and two grandchildren who reside with us and who might be placed at risk should this information be disseminated. I unequivocally do not want any of my personal information from Department of Corrections documents released to the ACLU. The release of this information would jeopardize my safety and the safety of my family.

Further Affiant Sayeth Not."

The document was signed and notarized on July 21, 2015.

In addition to the affidavits, there were letters prepared and sent, and an excerpt from one is as follows:

"July 24, 2015

I believe that, based on both Constitutional and common law, and as defined by the Merriam-Webster dictionary, the right to privacy is: the qualified legal right of a person to have reasonable privacy in not having his private affairs made known or his likeness exhibited to the public having regard to his habits, mode of living, and occupation.

Disclosure of my personal information as requested by the ACLU clearly would violate these rights, as well as my rights to seclusion, privacy and confidentiality. All of these were expectations when I provided this information to the Missouri Department of Corrections and remain as such.

As I understand it, the ACLU gathers this information on behalf of their client, Roderick Nunley (sic) with whom this information will be shared. Nunley is a convicted murderer with a prior history of convictions for various crimes and has spent the last 26 years associating with criminals while incarcerated. There is no guarantee that Nunley will not provide my personal information to others who may assist him in potential retaliation against me, my family, personal identity and/or personal property. My rights to safety, privacy, and protection against being another of Nunley's victims cannot be guaranteed."

The ACLU was more interested in the rights of convicted violent offenders than in those of honest, hardworking taxpayers who disagree with their political posturing. Under the Sunshine Law, their bid for personal information cast a dark and looming shadow over the Harrisons. It forced them to testify in a courtroom once again, reliving all the horror that had plagued them for decades. It was cruel and unusual punishment being meted out by the very group who claimed to oppose such suffering. It was unnecessary and unbearable to observe.

The attorney for the ACLU obviously failed to conduct the due diligence that one would expect a lawyer to perform, especially in a case that they started. When he began to question one of the witnesses, he began by asking, "Didn't you write a book about Ann Harrison?" It came as a surprise to him when the response was emphatical, "No." He looked at his notes, reading aloud a title, asking again, "Are you not the author?" Again, the response was unexpected. "Yes, but the book is not about Ann Harrison." The book he referenced was a true crime story, but it had nothing to do with the Ann Harrison case, nor was she mentioned anywhere in its text.

The first rule of trial lawyers is never to ask a question you don't already know the answer to, and one can only surmise that he must have been absent from law school the day that maxim was covered in class.

For whatever their intentions were, the ACLU's legal wrangling was simply grandstanding. No more, no less. They had searched the Internet to find out personal information already, the book issue being a case in point. Before testifying, the witnesses had already conducted their own computer searches and could find the requisite information the ACLU claimed they needed. The belief that executions would not occur without witnesses was heartless and misguided.

The ACLU accomplished nothing besides inconveniencing the witnesses and clogging the court with yet another frivolous case. There would still be representatives for Ann Harrison, who would bear witness to the execution of Roderick Nunley, notwithstanding. At the age of 50, Roderick Nunley would still die by lethal injection, and the witnesses would still attend the execution.

CHAPTER 23

If revenge is a dish best served cold, then what can be said of retribution? After twenty-five years of sitting raw and unaddressed, would it be like a plate of meat left to rot? Was there a stench left lingering that caught your breath and left you gasping, struggling to stay alive like fragments of what Ann endured in her dying moments? Was this a dish of bitter herbs reminiscent of the bitterness, poison, and death that Nunley and Taylor caused? If this was to be a judgment upon Roderick Nunley, would the retribution satiate the longing for justice for the victim?

At five minutes before 7:00 p.m., representatives from the prison announced that the State had lifted the stay on Roderick Nunley's execution. As a result, witnesses could go back to their cars, if necessary, as long as they went back through the metal detector. Food was made available, and they could eat. These were all significant, positive changes in the process for how victim families and witnesses were treated.

When Roderick Nunley was finally executed, Bob and Janel Harrison elected to release one final statement.

"For the last 26 years, Janel and I have, on occasion, experienced a form of compassion for not only Roderick Nunley and Michael Taylor, but especially their families. No one involved deserved the pain, suffering or anguish these two cowards have bestowed on this community. This feeling diminishes rapidly as our thoughts are uncontrollably

diverted to the vision of Ann being dragged into the stolen car by her hair and stomped to the floorboard in an attempt to hide her from sight as they transported her to Nunley's home. Upon arrival at the home, she was made to crawl through the garage to an area where the true torture began, not only physical, but mental. They recounted in their confessions that while she was blindfolded (sic) they laughed as she pleaded for her life and how they stood over her and discussed that they had to kill her so she could not identify them. Ann was then lifted into the trunk of the stolen car as Nunley went to the kitchen to obtain the murder weapons. After attempting to slit her throat, only to find the kitchen knives were too dull, they elected to stab her repeatedly in the chest and back and shut the trunk lid, only to hear her sobbing and moaning in her final moments of life.

Will the execution of Roderick Nunley and Michael Taylor bring a sense of closure for us and our younger daughters?

We don't know.

Will it put the heartbreak of reliving what they did to Ann during all the hearings, appeals and seemingly endless stalling attempts?

We certainly hope so.

If this is the only form of closure we receive, then we will gladly take it.

We want to express our deepest appreciation for all the support we have continuously received from our family, extended family, friends, Ann's classmates, The Raytown Girls Softball League, The National Center for Missing and Exploited Children, Governor Nixon, The Attorney General's office, the Department of Corrections and especially to the officers and detectives of the KCPD who worked tirelessly to bring Ann's killers to justice.

Finally, we wish to thank the many members of the media and press many of which have been at our side from the very morning Ann was taken. You have accepted the times when we were completely drained and just unable to speak to anyone. You allowed us the privacy we needed to work through the 26 years of grieving.

Thank you all,

Bob and Janel Harrison"

Unfortunately, the *Kansas City Star* elected to publish an article that selectively chose excerpts from the statement that gave the impression that the Harrisons were sympathetic to the Nunley and Taylor families and that all had been forgiven. This report was not the case, and public sentiment was against the paper, with an outcry for a retraction and apology. This article was an awful thing to wake up to the morning after the execution. It was just another cruel and unnecessary blow to a couple deserving of sympathy and support.

Radio talk show host, Dana Wright, was concerned enough to E-mail the newspaper about its spin that changed the context of the Harrisons' statement. "The first paragraph of the family statement makes it sound like the Harrison family is letting these guys off the hook," she wrote.

In an attempt to mitigate the damage, the *Star* posted the letter in its entirety. Still, it was stuck in the editorial section of the newspaper's webpage, where a reader would have to look for it to read the complete document. So, it was prefaced with the following, taken directly from that site:

"This is a place where the limitless space of the Web makes it possible both to quote from it and to publish the full text."

Shamefully, the full letter never appeared in any print edition of that newspaper.

Ann's killers remained on death row for over a quarter of a century. In stark contrast, Ann's young life spanned only 5,000 days. Yet, in those days, she radiated a light that could not be dimmed. Ann was a shy, beautiful girl who made a positive impression on all who knew her. Ann was an honor student, a star athlete, a talented musician, an animal lover, and a loyal friend. Ann was a loving daughter, granddaughter, sister, niece, cousin, and an innocent child of God.

On March 22, 1989, Ann was in her rightful place at the right time, simply waiting for a school bus. Ann was sixty-five feet from her own front door. There, but for the grace of God, stood any of us.

For twenty-six years, Ann's family was painfully forced to re-live the events of this case over and over as the result of frivolous appeals and demands from organizations that tout "civil liberties" but represent the victimizers and not the victims. Then, inexplicably, the scales of justice seemed to tip in favor of the killers, giving new meaning to the term "criminal justice." The remarkable team of detectives, prosecutors, and victim advocates rode the waves of emotional highs and lows with the family, waiting for the case they worked so vigorously to come to its just conclusion.

Nunley's execution was less justice and more retribution; it is a judgment upon the merciless who showed no mercy to Ann as she begged for her life. But despite what the *Kansas City Star* had inferred, their convictions were not biased sentences. On the contrary, the punishments meted out were befitting the heinous crimes intentionally perpetrated by two grown men against an innocent child: no more, no less.

The *Star* missed opportunities to do something powerful by informing citizens of how their tax dollars are being wasted repeatedly by defense attorneys clutching at baseless claims. Instead, the same empty arguments were filed countless times and denied by the courts. At some point, there needs to be an expectation that the courts will say "enough is enough" and cease permitting the re-victimization of the families who have already borne a cross for sins they did not commit.

Newspapers like the *Star* could inform the public of what contemporary death row inmates actually experience. For example, in Missouri, they do not sit in solitary confinement for twenty-three hours each day. Instead, they live in the general population with access to televisions, computers, a gym, and, unfortunately, all the sex, drugs, and other illicit items they can manage to procure. Moreover, an inmate is only moved to solitary for thirty days before execution.

Compelling images such as tragic solitary confinement with its wretched loneliness, an apologetic and recompensed Birdman of Alcatraz, or the sympathetic soul of the miraculous John Coffey, "like the drink, except not spelled the same," spring from the vivid imaginations of creative scriptwriters. But unfortunately, it is simply the genre of Hollywood hype, and it would be a service if the public knew this.

Informing its readers, telling them the truth about the prison system, exposing its dark and ugly underbelly—this is the stuff deserving of Pulitzer Prizes. But unfortunately, society seems to lack reporters with the level of ethics, both work and personal, required to undertake this and expose the truth.

There is an epitaph from an old European Monastery that reads,

> *"Remember friend as you walk by*
> *As you are now so once was I*
> *As I am now you will surely be*
> *Prepare thyself to follow me."*

Whether prepared or not, the remaining killer of Ann Marie Harrison had, after twenty-six years, finally followed her to his own death. As with his crime partner before him, the State of Missouri provided a quiet, secure, and painless end to his existence, a dignity not afforded to his victim. Despite being brutalized, tortured, and stabbed, she waged one final, valiant struggle against her merciless captors before she succumbed to her injuries. Ann Harrison did not go gently into that good night.

CHAPTER 24

In August of 2015, Nunley's daughter submitted an affidavit to the Missouri Supreme Court on behalf of her father, stating that she would be willing to serve as her father's next friend in litigation. "Next Friend" is a legal definition describing a person acting on behalf of an infant or other person under legal disability. Nunley clearly met the definition.

During his execution, Nunley's breathing became heavy for a few seconds. Then, he briefly opened his mouth before becoming still. He was pronounced dead at 9:09 p.m. CDT. Of twenty executions nationally in 2015, ten had been in Texas, and Nunley's made the sixth death row inmate to be put to death in Missouri.

It was never disclosed whether or not anyone from his family attended the execution or even claimed his body.

The following is an excerpt from the statement issued by the Missouri Dept. of Corrections spokesman Mike O'Connell:

"Roderick Nunley was executed by lethal injection at 8:58 p.m. on Tuesday, Sept. 1, 2015 at the Eastern Reception, Diagnostic and Correctional Center in Bonne Terre, Missouri for the 1989 murder of Ann Harrison in Jackson County. He was pronounced dead at 9:09 p.m.

His last meal was a steak, shrimp, chicken strips, salad and a slice of cheesecake."

After Nunley's execution, Missouri Department of Corrections Director, George A. Lombardi, read the following statement from Gov. Jay Nixon:

"Tonight, as we remember Ann Harrison, our thoughts and prayers are again with Bob and Janel Harrison, and the other members of Ann's family. The acts of violence that took this 15-year-old who was full of life and promise away from her loved ones can never make sense to us.

The two men who were found guilty of Ann's kidnapping, rape and murder have now had their sentences carried out. But even as there is judicial closure tonight, we know that a Missouri family will always miss and grieve the young woman who has been gone for more than 26 years. We grieve with them.

So, I ask that Missourians join me in keeping the family of Ann Harrison in their thoughts and prayers tonight."

Roderick Nunley did not provide a final statement to anyone before his execution.

✳

Before Nunley's execution, Lisa Harrison posted a message on Facebook.

"I've spent the past couple months creating a mental draft of what I would want to say for Nunley's execution. I could write about the emotional roller coaster I experienced last year with Taylor's execution. I could write about closure and being unsure if that is something I will experience and to what extent. I could thank the hundreds of people who have supported our family much like I did last year. I could share the heartache of the past 26 years, or I could share how thankful I am to have had such strong parents and sister to show me how to cope and be a stronger person.

I stayed up until 3 am (sic) writing, draft after draft, trying to find words that can express exactly how I felt. I woke up at 6 this morning to my son climbing up on me, ready to watch TV and get the day started. He could sense something was up. I was my usual sleepy self, but I clearly wasn't in the mood for his overly excited demeanor. He would demand I get up off the couch and do puzzles. He would manage to find finger paint and insist he wanted to paint. He would pull a book for me to read, get dressed in his astronaut suit and request that we watch Apollo 13. He would try to motivate me to clean the house and be productive somehow. He wasn't about to let me sleep all day as I wait for 6 o'clock tonight.

I was his age when Ann died.

I would spend more time looking at the same photos I have of us. I don't have many, but I have studied the same batch of photos for the past 26 years. Easter, 1988. Studio portraits, 1986-1988. Halloween, 1988. My birthday, 1989.

Finally, a picture of me sitting at her gravesite.

This one photograph sums up every feeling I have today. I don't think I could possibly put into words everything this photograph means to me. The hours we spent there, riding my bike, picking up flowers before the groundskeeper mowed. The innocence that I had. The months using my Mickey Mouse phone to try to call Ann. I was convinced E.T. had taken her and I wanted to know when she would come home.

I know I am not alone today as we all wait for 6 o'clock. I went back and forth on if I wanted to share my thoughts today or keep them to myself. Call me superstitious, but publicly sharing my emotions last year for the first time in my life ended with Taylor's execution taking place. It can't hurt to do it again."

CHAPTER 25

Debra Harrison learned to play the flute on the same instrument that Ann had used. It was the instrument left behind on the curb in front of the Harrison home when Ann was abducted, the one that lay by her side in her casket at her wake. It was painful at times for her parents to hear the music in their house. Hauntingly beautiful, yet tragically sad.

Ann left a legacy of friendships that carry forward to this day. For decades, Janel Harrison maintained a close friendship with David Schesser's mother, Elena. With significant health problems that mandated long-term care, Janel served as Elena's driver, accompanying her to doctor's appointments, regularly visiting her care facility, helping her as any friend would until the day she died. Likewise, Ann's best friend, Juliet, remains close to Ann's parents, spending time with the Harrisons, staying with them at their cabin at the Lake of the Ozarks, sharing her own daughter with them as extended family. It is a fitting tribute to the type of people that the Harrison family comprises.

The Harrisons continued to remain in the family home after Ann's death. They were fixtures in their community. Both daughters, Debra and Lisa, attended Raytown schools. It was still home for the Harrisons, but with it came a price. There would always be the "aren't you Ann's mother?" or the look that came over someone's face when they recalled, "My daughter went to school with yours" that seemed less often to be a recollection of the two younger girls and more of a veiled attempt to identify with Ann's parents.

The uneasiness was palpable—the foot shuffling, the stammering, the "I do not know what to say" pauses in conversation. Friends could see it, so it had to be evident to the couple who wanted to keep Ann's memory alive but maintain a balance because they still had a life with two beautiful, vibrant girls who were the center of their world.

Sometimes people would ask about the entire family, but the memories of that tragic time still could take up all the oxygen in a room. It was unsettling, but it was the way life was. It was not normal. For the Harrisons, normal was nothing more than a dryer setting, and all the "at least you have closure" and "she's in a better place" well-intentioned comments could not change the fact that they were paying a king's ransom for a crime they did not commit, a debt they did not owe. The demons which plagued the Harrisons' dreams were real, so waiting almost three decades for the execution of the sentence imposed and the termination of the lives of Ann's murderers seemed far too great a span of time.

※

For twenty-three years, the Raytown softball league in which Ann played, held a fundraising tournament in her honor. So, when the Harrisons decided it was time to bring to closure a Raytown tradition after almost a quarter of a century, it was bittersweet. However, Ann loved to play softball. The annual event held in her honor afforded both Ann's close family—and the community who rallied on behalf of her—an opportunity to celebrate her life.

Equally significant was the benefit it served the Lost Child Network—now the Center for Missing and Exploited Children—raising much-needed funds to support their mission. When the tournament program was disbanded,

Craig Hill, one of the Center's founders, and a member of the Leawood Police Department, crafted the following letter:

"2012

As Father's Day weekend approaches, I wanted to take a minute to thank everyone who has supported this great tournament and cause over the past 23 years. The Harrison family has asked that we discontinue the tournament, and we are honoring their wishes.

I've had the honor and privilege to be the tournament director for this tournament the past three years and I've met some very giving and caring people over those three years. This tournament always seemed to bring the best out of everyone involved... players, coaches, umpires, parents, volunteers, etc. It was one of my favorite weekends of the year.

Special thanks also to some of the young ladies who have volunteered their time to come help out... I'm sure I'll miss a few so I apologize in advance... but thanks to Joella Vauthier, Caitlyn Shireman, Mackenzie Ryle, Brenna Hubbard and Audrey White for all your help during the tournament.

The purpose of this tournament was to remember Ann Harrison and also raise money (in Ann's name) for the Center for Missing and Exploited Children. It's my hope that the thousands and thousands of dollars donated as a result of this tournament helped keep our children safe... if one life was saved because of the programs this tournament helped fund, it was all worthwhile.

Thanks again to all who helped support this tournament during my three years and the countless others who made this tournament a success for the 20 years prior. We have an amazing softball community here in Kansas since the first time I met Bob and Janel Harrison as President of The Lost Child Network, I have had the privilege of working with them since that tragic day they lost their daughter, Ann Marie, in 1989 (sic).

Over the past 23 years, this wonderful couple played a major role in the growth of many prevention educational programs as well as the construction of the NCMEC (National Center for Missing & Exploited Children) Kansas City Branch Child Resource Center, named in honor of their daughter.

As you all are aware, it did not stop there. Every single year, regardless of the weather, the remarkable friends from the Raytown Softball League, tournament organizers, coaches, umpires, players, and their families & friends brought together a Kansas City tradition with the Ann Marie Harrison Annual Girls Softball tournament benefiting the National Center for Missing & Exploited Children.

With close to $140,000 raised, the donations and funds generated from the Ann Marie Harrison Tournament were used specifically for scheduling law enforcement trainings, prevention education presentations and Photofacts ID events-the sole focus being how to keep our children safe and assisting law enforcement agencies with needed training & materials.

The support given by the softball community in the Kansas City and surrounding areas to the National Center for Missing & Exploited Children the last 23 years deserves so much more than just a thank you. Because of Bob and Janel Harrison, thousands of children were able to learn how to be safe. Now as grown-ups, they can pass those messages on to their own kids.

God Bless Bob and Janel Harrison

Craig Hill

Associate Director of Training & Outreach

National Center for Missing & Exploited Children

✲

The executions of the killers of Ann Marie Harrison are now old news, but Ann's purpose-filled life left an enduring legacy of love and joy to all who knew her. Her closest friends have remained an active part of the lives of Bob and Janel Harrison, a tribute to the love and generosity Ann's parents have shown in the face of unfathomable suffering. Fundraisers in her honor have provided over $140,000 to the Center for Missing and Exploited Children. Laws affording victims and their families to give impact statements have been enacted because of this case. The Harrisons have been active and impactful members of organizations such as Parents of Murdered Children and The Lost Child Network, serving as an inspiration to others who have had to deal with the violent death of a child through no fault of their own. In her memory, volunteers helped build a rose garden at the Cave Springs Interpretive Center just down the road from the cemetery where Ann was laid to rest. A remembrance celebration was held there for the 25th anniversary of Ann's death. Friends from Raytown South High School, community members, and the family spoke. The tributes were heartfelt and genuine, reflecting the impact Ann made on the lives she touched.

CHAPTER 26

No one can truly understand the everlasting impact such a violent crime has on those close to it. The chain of events that resulted from Michael Taylor's decision to grab Ann Harrison and force her into a stolen car that March morning was unforeseen and unavoidable. It was that perfect storm that brought forth a deluge of suffering and horror that rained down on everyone who came in contact with the case.

Investigating a violent death of an innocent victim—no matter the age, sex, race, religion, or sexual orientation—takes a tremendous toll on the detectives, district officers, crime scene investigators, dispatchers, all the responders who in whatever manner touch the case.

Detective Matthew Rog worked on Ann's case from the night the police discovered her body until it was solved. He candidly shared his experience, an event that remains with him even today.

It was early evening on March 23, 1989. He had been working days on Murder Squad, handling active cases where there was no known suspect. He would continue to follow up on leads until they "caught a new one," which was KCPD Homicide-speak for another murder in the city. The Murder Squad kept 7:00 a.m.-3:00 p.m. hours but, when called out to a new crime scene, they would respond 24/7. He was eating dinner with his family when his department-issued pager rang. Rog was notified by the dispatcher to respond to an address on South Ditman Avenue without delay. Dispatch offered no further information.

When he arrived at the scene, it was clear that this was more than just a call-out for a new murder case. There were police cars, marked and unmarked, arriving at the scene. Officers gathered around a blue Chevrolet Monte Carlo parked in front of the address. The trunk was open and, as he approached the vehicle, he could see a body. His first thought was, "Oh, my God. It must be Ann Harrison."

As detectives worked the case, they would visit and revisit locations for any potential witnesses. All reports would be scrutinized, and additional focus would be placed on similar crimes in the area; burglaries and auto thefts were of particular interest. At first, everything was speculation with no witnesses, no weapon, no crime scene other than the trunk of the Monte Carlo. Frustration set in, but detectives had resolved that they would solve Ann's case sooner rather than later.

"Looking into the trunk of that car on that night will haunt me until the day I die," he would say, some thirty years later.

There were scores of people who volunteered to search for Ann's killers, but detectives were at a loss about where willing community members could begin to initiate a search. Officers had already gone to prominent locations, places close to the recovered stolen auto where the child's body was found; vacant areas and parks between the Harrisons' address and Ditman Avenue were logical choices, but from which direction?

Scores of psychic predictions came in, most of which indicated that she was in the water or an abandoned building. Someone even brought in "psychic dogs," which they claimed could find the crime scene. The potential for that was quickly dispelled by detectives who humored the unsuccessful efforts of the handlers. It forced officers to squander precious time as it proved to be a farce, but it still needed to be followed up. Edlund and his detectives would leave no stone unturned, nor permit potential criticism from observers by not acting on leads, no matter how foolish or unrealistic these proved to be.

Rog would later describe the personal impact of a case such as Ann Harrison's on those charged with investigating and solving the crime.

"I had nightmares about it. Many a night, I would wake up in a cold sweat and sit straight up in bed, seeing her in the trunk. I would wonder what else could I have done to find her. Could I have looked just one more place? You feel a lot of misplaced guilt from a case like this."

Rog used his private vehicle and searched for hours, driving around South Zone, an area he was intimately familiar with from the years he worked there, using his knowledge, hoping to find some elusive clue.

His response to Ann's case mirrored the comments offered by other detectives interviewed about the case, how they used their own time to run down leads, the sleepless nights replaying the day's events, grasping for one more clue that might bring closure to this case.

The command staff did their best to not micro-manage the investigative team, which was just as well, as Van Buskirk would never have allowed it anyway. Instead, he stood steadfast in his oversight of violent crime cases, commanding the respect of those he worked for and those who worked for him.

Only those who walk the walk and talk the talk day-in-and-day-out honestly know what first responders and members of law enforcement go through. As President Theodore Roosevelt so eloquently stated,

"It is not the critic who counts; not the man who points out how the strong man stumbles, or where the doer of deeds could have done them better. The credit belongs to the man who is actually in the arena, whose face is marred by dust

and sweat and blood; who strives valiantly; who errs, who comes short again and again, because there is no effort without error and shortcoming; but who does actually strive to do the deeds; who knows great enthusiasms, the great devotions; who spends himself in a worthy cause; who at the best knows in the end the triumph of high achievement, and who at the worst, if he fails, at least fails while daring greatly, so that his place shall never be with those cold and timid souls who neither know victory nor defeat."

CHAPTER 27

Ann Marie Harrison's resting place is high on a spot in Mount Olivet Cemetery, near cedar trees whose roots are shallow and thrive where others cannot. Like the hardy cedars, Ann Marie Harrison's legacy thrives, not only in the hearts of those who loved her but in the memories of the scores of law enforcement officers who searched for her and in the history of a community that mourned for her. Native Americans, primarily the Cherokee, believe that cedar trees hold special powers to protect their loved ones from evil and that the spirits of their dearly departed are held within their branches. Forever green, the cedars of Mount Olivet stand guard and protect Ann from the evil spirits that folklore claimed walked the earth.

It was never shared with the witnesses what actually became of the bodies of the two men who murdered Ann Harrison. According to the staff who worked at the prison, it was anticipated that Nunley's body would not be taken by the family; therefore, he would be buried by the State of Missouri according to the prison's policies on deceased prisoners. The disposition of Taylor's body was unknown.

And their sun does never shine,
And their fields are bleak and bare,
And their ways are filled with thorns;
It is eternal winter there.

Excerpt from the poem *Holy Thursday* by William Blake

Ann Marie Harrison's light still shines, and its warmth can be felt by all those whose lives she touched. May she rest in peace in the arms of angels.

AFTERWORD

When something as unexplainable as the abduction and murder of an innocent young girl happens, one unanswered question continues to surface: it begs the answer to why would a loving God allow this to happen? Arguing the existence of evil is in line with arguing about the existence of God. When bad things happen to good people, we question the latter, wondering how events like the murder of Ann Harrison could ever occur. Thomas Aquinas said, "Good can exist without evil, whereas evil cannot exist without good. Conversely, good can live independently, with nothing counter to sustain it. It allows us to take comfort in knowing that good continues to exist, even if it is often overshadowed by evil.

Like water and air, evil is clear, colorless, formless, with no sense of taste or smell to warn us of its presence. Yet, as air and water are essential to life, evil brings with it actions that can cause the termination of life, the cessation of happiness, the end of much goodness. Its companions are deadly sins, broken commandments, violated laws.

For myself, evil is like a thin piece of glass, offering no warning as we come upon it, stopping us in our tracks when we try to pass through it. When it shatters from the weight of our being, it cuts us with the vainest slivers, leaving us to bleed, whether literally as in Ann's case or figuratively, carving pain into our very souls.

The learned will argue that God did not create evil, only good, and that evil is a consequence of free will. As one who has remained close to this case for a very long time, I like that interpretation. Contemplating Taylor and Nunley's actions, it is clear that they acted upon their own desires, relying upon their own free will and decision-making to take a life, hide the evidence, and, when finally confronted with their crimes, to sign consent forms and confess voluntarily.

Ironically, and in stark contrast to its intended goal, evil gives us a measure for goodness. The crimes committed against Ann Harrison made her light shine even brighter, drawing attention to the quiet virtue that she represented, the righteous indignation of a community, the integrity of law enforcement, and the ultimate realization of justice.

Evil is a four-letter word. Hope, love, heal are also four-letter words. And, as we have seen by the life of Ann Marie Harrison, so too is the word "good."

—The Author

*

Where does anyone begin to thank all the individuals who stepped forward to search for Ann, search for her killers, and search for justice? Please know that there are no words to fully express the gratitude felt for all those who touched this case, directly or indirectly, whether through actions, words, or prayers.

With sincerest appreciation, a special thanks to just a few of those who demonstrated the courage to stand in the arena:

Chief Larry Joiner (retired) and the officers and employees of the Kansas City, Missouri Police Department (current & retired)

The Grandview Police Department

The Raytown Police Department

The Missouri Highway Patrol

Missouri Search and Rescue K-9 Unit
The Jackson County Sheriff's Department
The Jackson County Parks Department
Gary Van Buskirk
Pete Edlund
Troy Cole
Al De Valkenaere
Victor Zinn
Ed Glynn
William R. Martin
Bill Wilson
Joe Chapman
Reed Buente
Bill McGhee
Matt Rog
William Wilson
Garry Wantland
Chris Jefferson
Rick Pilgrim
Herb Acklin
The Harrison Family
Danny & Jenelle Meng
Office of the Director - Missouri Department of Corrections
Office of Victim Services - Missouri Department of Corrections
Warden and Staff - Eastern Reception, Diagnostic and Correctional Center

Legal Chronology for Michael Taylor

1989

March 22 – Michael Taylor and co-defendant Roderick Nunley kidnap, rape, and murder 15-year-old Ann Harrison.

June 23 – Michael Taylor confesses to killing Ann Harrison.

July 28 – The state charges Taylor by indictment with first degree murder, forcible rape, kidnapping, and armed criminal action.

1991

February 8 – Taylor pleads guilty to the charges.

April 23 – The penalty phase begins before the circuit court.

May 3 – The Jackson County Circuit Court sentences Taylor to death for the murder conviction, life for the rape conviction, 15 years for the kidnapping conviction, and life for the armed criminal action conviction.

May 13 – Taylor files a notice of appeal.

August 9 – Taylor files a Rule 24.035 motion for post-conviction relief in the Jackson County Circuit Court.

1992

July 1 – The Circuit Court denies post-conviction relief.

1993

June 29 – The Missouri Supreme Court remands for a new sentencing proceeding.

1994

May 2 – The second penalty phase begins.

June 17 – The Jackson County Circuit Court sentences Taylor to death for the murder conviction, 15 years for the kidnapping conviction, life for the rape conviction, and 50 years for the armed criminal action conviction, the sentences to run consecutively.

September 15 – Taylor files a Rule 24.034 motion for post-conviction relief in the Jackson County Circuit Court.

1995

June 20 – The Circuit Court denies post-conviction relief.

1996

August 2 – The Missouri Supreme Court affirms Taylor's conviction and sentence and the denial of post-conviction relief. State v. Taylor, 929 S.W.2d 209 (Mo.banc 1996).

1997

February 24 – The United States Supreme Court denies certiorari review. Taylor v. Missouri, 519 U.S.1152(1997).

1998

February 23 – Taylor files a petition for writ of habeas corpus in the United States District Court of the Western District Missouri.

2000

July 10 – The District Court denies the petition for writ of habeas corpus in an unpublished order.

2003

August 18 – The Court of Appeals affirms the denial of habeas corpus relief. Taylor v. Bowersox, 329 F.3d 963 (8th Cir. 2003).

2004

March 22 – The Supreme Court denies discretionary review. Taylor v. Bowersox, 541 U.S. 947 (2004).

2005

June 3 – Taylor files civil suit challenging constitutionality of lethal injection as method of execution.

2006

January 31 – The United States District Court for the Western District of Missouri finds lethal injection is constitutional.

February 1 – The Court of Appeals issues a stay of execution pending review of district court decision. The Supreme Court upholds the stay. Crawford v. Nixon, 126 S.Ct. 1192 (2006) April 11 – The Missouri Supreme Court issues writ to Jackson County Circuit Court prohibiting it from reopening Rule 24.035 litigation. State ex rel. Nixon v. Daugherty, 186 S.W.3d 253 (Mo. band 2006)

April 27 – The Court of Appeals retains jurisdiction and remands to district court for further hearing. Taylor v. Crawford, 445 F.3d 1095 (8th Cir. 2006)

June 26 – The district court finds Missouri's method of execution unconstitutional and suggests changes to improve it. Taylor v. Crawford, 2006 WL 1779035 (W.D. Mo2006)

August 9 – The Court of Appeals relinquishes jurisdiction to district court. Taylor v. Crawford, 457 F. 3d 902 (8th Cir. 2006)

September 12 – The district court finds Missouri's written protocol unconstitutional.

2007

June 4 – The Court of Appeals reverses district court judgement and finds the written protocol constitutional. Taylor v. Crawford, 487 F.3d 1072 (8th Cir. 2007)

2008

May 20 – The Missouri Supreme Court affirms the denial of post-conviction relief by the Jackson County Circuit Court. Taylor v. State, 254 S.W.3d 856 (Mo. band 2008)

2009

February 24 – The Missouri Supreme Court rejects a claim by Taylor and others that written protocol did not conform to state law. Middleton v. Missouri Department of Corrections, 278 S.W.3d 193 (Mo. band 2009)

November 10 – The Court of Appeals for the Eighth Circuit concludes the protocol is applied constitutionally. Clemons v. Crawford, 585 F.3d 1119 (8th Cir. 2009)

2011

May 31 – The Missouri Supreme Court rejects Taylor's challenge to judge sentencing. State ex del. Taylor v. Steele, 341 S.W.3rd 634 (Mo.banc 2011)

Legal Chronology for Roderick Nunley

1989

March 22 – Michael Taylor and co-defendant Roderick Nunley kidnap, rape, and murder 15-year-old Ann Harrison.

July 28 – A grand jury in Jackson County indicts Nunley for first-degree murder, armed criminal action, kidnapping, and forcible rape.

1990

June 1 – The Jackson County Prosecutor files an information in lieu of indictment charging Nunley as a prior and persistent offender.

Sept. 27 – Request for change of judge filed by Nunley seeking to remove Judge Levitt in Division 13.

Oct. 2 – Case moved to Division 14.

Oct. 10 – State successfully moves for change of judge. The case is sent to Division II — Judge Donald L. Mason.

Oct. 24 – Judge Mason disqualifies himself and the case is reassigned to Division 4 — Judge Alvin Randall.

1991

Jan 28 – Nunley pleads guilty to Judge Randall.

May 31 – Judge Randall sentences Nunley to death.

Aug. 12 – Nunley files a pro se Rule 24.035 motion.

Sept. 3 – Judge Randall recuses himself from the Rule 24.035 case (Apparently upon learning the amended motion would accuse him of drinking before sentencing).

Oct. 9 – Judge Randall recuses himself from the criminal and Rule 24.035 cases.

Oct. 15 – Nunley files an amended Rule 24.035 motion alleging Judge Randall was drinking before sentencing.

Oct. 28 – Judge Mauer recuses himself. Judge Mason, presiding judge, purports to recuse all judges in the 16th Judicial Circuit.

Nov. 22 – The Missouri Supreme Court appoints Judge Robert H. Dierker from the 22nd Judicial Circuit to handle the case.

1992

Jan. 3 – Hearing held on Rule 24.035 motion.

March 23 – Hearing held on Rule 24.035 motion.

March 26 – Hearing held on Rule 24.035 motion.

July 1 – Judge Dierker denies Rule 24.35 motion.

1993

June 29 – The Missouri Supreme Court remands the case for a new penalty phase.

Dec. 27 – Nunley moves to withdraw guilty plea.

1994

Jan. 26 – Hearing on motion to withdraw guilty plea before Judge O'Malley.

Feb. 3 – Judge O'Malley denies motion to withdraw guilty plea.

May 10 – Judge O'Malley sentences Nunley to death.

July 13 – Nunley files pro se Rule 24.035 motion.

Oct. 10 – Nunley files amended motion for post-conviction relief.

Dec. 21 – Hearing held on Rule 24.035 motion.

1995

Feb. 14 – Hearing held on Rule 24.035 motion. March 16, Judge O'Malley denies Rule 24.035 motion.

1996

March 28 – The Missouri Supreme Court affirms in part, but remands for additional findings.

Nov. 20 – Judge O'Malley denies the additional Rule 24.035 claims.

1997

Jan. 21 – The United States Supreme Court denies certiorari on the first Missouri Supreme Court decision.

1998

Nov. 3 – The Missouri Supreme Court affirms the denial of post-conviction relief.

1999

May 3 – The United States Supreme Court denies certiorari on the second Missouri Supreme Court decision.

2000

April 28 – A federal habeas petition is filed in the United States District Court for the Western District of Missouri.

2003

June 5 – The United States District Court denies the petition for habeas corpus.

June 16 – Nunley files motion to alter or amend.

Dec. 4 – The United State District Court denies the motion to alter or amend.

2005

Jan. 14 – The United States Court of Appeals for the Eighth Circuit affirms the denial of habeas corpus.

Oct. 3 – The United States Supreme Court denies certiorari.

2010

Aug. 19 – The Missouri Supreme Court issues an execution warrant for Nunley and sets the execution date for Oct. 20, 2010.

Sept. 30 – The Missouri Supreme Court denies stay application.

Oct. 12 – The Missouri Supreme Court denies motion to recall mandate and stay application.

Oct. 18 – The United States District Court for the Western District of Missouri stays the execution based on the right to jury sentencing claim.

2011

May 31 - The Missouri Supreme Court denies habeas corpus petition in a published decision on jury sentencing claim.

2013

April 18 – The United States District Court for the Western District of Missouri denies the supplemental habeas corpus petition on the jury sentencing claim.

2014

March 12 – The United States District Court for the Western District of Missouri denies motion to vacate the stay of execution.

2015

April 27 – The United States Court of Appeals for the Eighth Circuit affirms the denial of the supplemental petition for habeas corpus.

June 15 – The United State Court of Appeals for the Eighth Circuit vacates the stay of execution.

July 6 – The Missouri Supreme Court issues an execution warrant for Nunley and sets the execution date for September 1, 2015.

PHOTOS

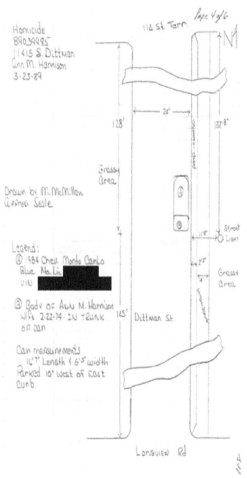

Crime Scene Drawing
Courtesy of the Kansas City, Missouri Police Department

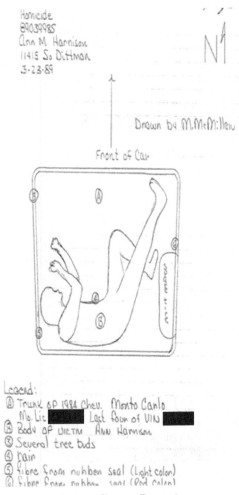

Homicide
89039985
Ann M. Harrison
11415 So. Dittman
3-23-89

N1

Drawn by M. McMillen

Front of Car

Legend:
Ⓐ Trunk of 1984 Chev. Monte Carlo
    No Lic ▓▓▓▓▓▓ Last four of VIN ▓▓▓▓▓
Ⓑ Body of victim Ann Harrison
Ⓒ Several tree buds
Ⓓ rain
Ⓔ fibre from rubber seal (light color)
Ⓕ fibre from rubber seal (Red Color)

Crime Scene Drawing
Courtesy of the Kansas City, Missouri Police Department

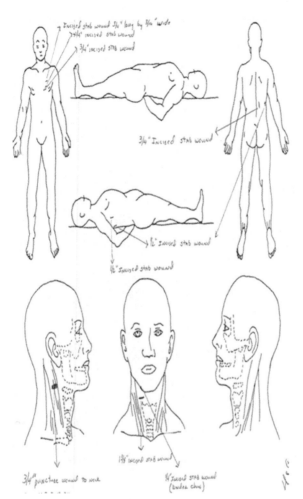

Crime Scene Drawing
Courtesy of the Kansas City, Missouri Police Department

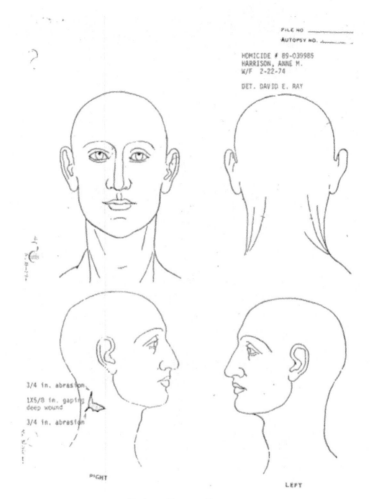

Crime Scene Drawing
Courtesy of the Kansas City, Missouri Police Department

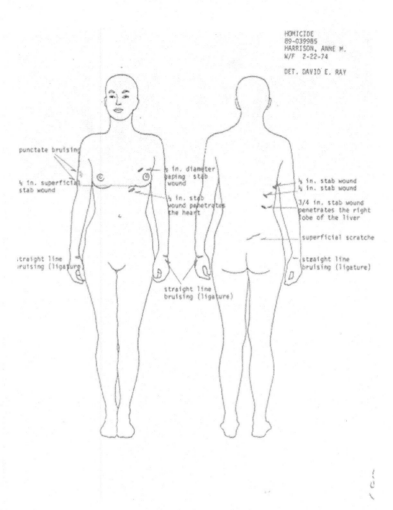

HOMICIDE
89-039985
HARRISON, ANNE M.
W/F 2-22-74

DET. DAVID E. RAY

punctate bruising

½ in. diameter
gaping stab
wound

½ in. superficial
stab wound

½ in. stab
wound penetrates
the heart

½ in. stab wound
½ in. stab wound

3/4 in. stab wound
penetrates the right
lobe of the liver

superficial scratche

straight line
bruising (ligature)

straight line
bruising (ligature)

straight line
bruising (ligature)

Crime Scene Drawing
Courtesy of the Kansas City, Missouri Police Department

7405 E. 118th Street
Courtesy of Google Earth

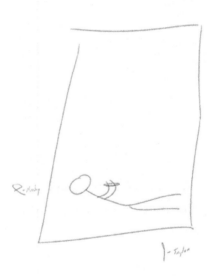

Taylor's Drawing of Ann in Car Trunk
Courtesy of the Kansas City, Missouri Police Department

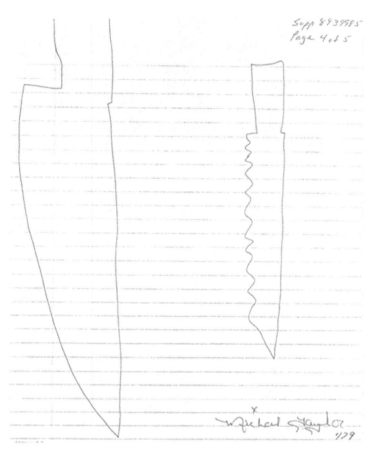

Taylor's Drawing of Murder Weapons
Courtesy of the Kansas City, Missouri Police Department

Ann Harrison and David Schesser
Courtesy of Bob and Janel Harrison

The Harrison Family
Courtesy of Bob and Janel Harrison

Lisa Harrison at Ann's Grave Site
Courtesy of Bob and Janel Harrison

Ann Marie Harrison
Courtesy of Bob and Janel Harrison

Michael Taylor
Courtesy of the Missouri Department of Corrections

Roderick Nunley
Courtesy of the Missouri Department of Corrections

Kareem Hurley
Courtesy of the Missouri Department of Corrections

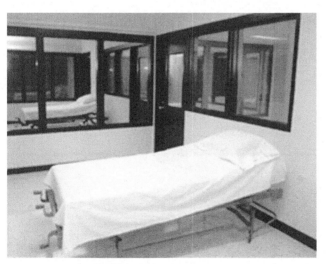

Missouri Death Chamber – Bonne Terre, Missouri
Courtesy of the Missouri Department of Corrections

*For More News About Marla Bernard,
Signup For Our Newsletter:*

http://wbp.bz/newsletter

*Word-of-mouth is critical to an author's long-
term success. If you appreciated this book please
leave a review on the Amazon sales page:*

http://wbp.bz/sideroad

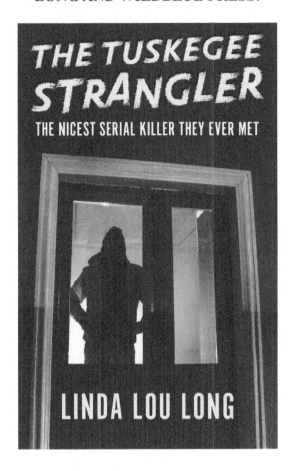

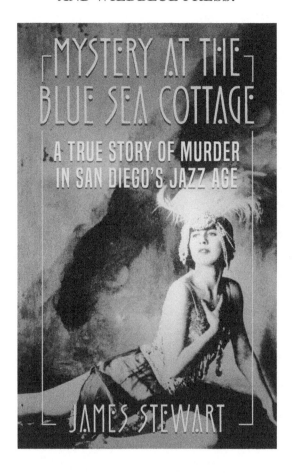

Made in the USA
Coppell, TX
22 May 2023

17175483R00134